MAPPING YOUR FUTURE

About the Author

Kris Brandt Riske, M.A., (Arizona) is a professional astrologer. She serves on the board of the National Council for Geocosmic Research, has a master's degree in journalism, and is the author of numerous articles for popular astrology magazines and publications. She was a contributor to *Civilization Under Attack*, has written annual weather forecasts for Llewellyn's *Moon Sign Book,* and has written articles and a weather forecast for Llewellyn's *Starview Almanac.*

To Write to the Author

If you wish to contact the author or would like more information about this book, please write to the author in care of Llewellyn Worldwide and we will forward your request. Both the author and publisher appreciate hearing from you and learning of your enjoyment of this book and how it has helped you. Llewellyn Worldwide cannot guarantee that every letter written to the author can be answered, but all will be forwarded. Please write to:

Kris Brandt Riske
⅝ Llewellyn Worldwide
P.O. Box 64383, Dept. 0-7387-0501-2
St. Paul, MN 55164-0383, U.S.A.

Please enclose a self-addressed stamped envelope for reply,
or $1.00 to cover costs. If outside U.S.A., enclose
international postal reply coupon.

Many of Llewellyn's authors have websites with additional information and resources. For more information, please visit our website at
http://www.llewellyn.com

MAPPING YOUR Future

Understand & Maximize Your Potential

Kris Brandt Riske, M.A.

2004
Llewellyn Publications
St. Paul, Minnesota 55164-0383, U.S.A.

First Edition
First Printing, 2004

Book design by Donna Burch
Cover art © DigitalVision & Digital Stock
Cover design by Kevin R. Brown
Edited by Andrea Neff

Chart wheels were produced by the Kepler program by permission of Cosmic Patterns Software, Inc. (www.AstroSoftware.com)

Library of Congress Cataloging-in-Publication Data

Riske, Kris Brandt.
  Mapping your future : understand and maximize your potential / Kris Brandt Riske.—1st ed.
    p.   cm.
  Includes bibliographical references.
  ISBN 0-7387-0501-2
    1. Predictive astrology. I. Title.

  BF1720.5.R57 2004
  133.5—dc22

                                                                              2004044120

Llewellyn Publications
A Division of Llewellyn Worldwide, Ltd.
P.O. Box 64383, Dept. 0-7387-0501-2
St. Paul, MN 55164-0383, U.S.A.
www.llewellyn.com

Printed in the United States of America

Other Books and Articles by Kris Brandt Riske, M.A.

Astrometeorology: Planetary Power in Weather Forecasting
American Federation of Astrologers, 1997

Civilization Under Attack (Co-author)
Llewellyn Publications, 2001

Llewellyn's Moon Sign Book (Contributor)
Llewellyn Publications, 2002, 2003, 2004

Forthcoming Books and Articles by Kris Brandt Riske, M.A.

Llewellyn's Moon Sign Book (Contributor)
Llewellyn Publications, 2005

Llewellyn's Starview Almanac (Contributor)
Llewellyn Publications, 2005

Mapping Your Money
Llewellyn Publications, 2005

To George Speck, my dear friend who made it happen

Contents

Ten

Eleven

Twelve

Thirteen

Fourteen

Charts

All chart data for celebrities and public figures came from AstroDatabank (www.astrodatabank.com). All chart data for anonymous case studies came from client files.

Acknowledgments

Many thanks to the Llewellyn team and most especially to editor Andrea Neff, for her astute observations and superb suggestions.

Thanks also to Fei and David Cochrane of Cosmic Patterns Software for creating the software CD that accompanies this book, and to the friends and clients who shared their stories and charts so that others could learn from their experiences.

Special thanks to Stephanie Clement for her inspiring and motivational words.

Introduction

Predictive astrology is a powerful tool that can help you optimize the strengths and talents promised by your birth chart. Knowing when to act, when not to upset the status quo, or when you're more likely to face challenges or receive gifts from the universe is invaluable information that can be gleaned by mapping your future.

What predictive astrology cannot do, however, is make choices; that is a matter of free will, a choice of one path over another. It's ultimately up to you. But predictive astrology can help you weigh the odds to make more informed choices about everything from marriage to buying a home to moving cross-country.

Think of predictive astrology not as fateful, but as a road map that helps you map out the shortest route to your goal. When you know what possibilities the future holds, you can better prepare yourself to take advantage of opportunities, or even put a positive spin on life's bumps in the road.

This book shows you the basic tools of predictive astrology and how to apply them to forecast trends and specific events. By following the step-by-step techniques, and studying the examples of everyday and well-known people, you can discover prime times to find love, go for a promotion, seek a new job, relocate, or hope for a windfall.

It's important to read the chapters in order because each builds on the previous one. Begin with your natal chart (birth chart), which is the foundation of predictive astrology. Discover the best in you, as well as stumbling blocks to be overcome. The more you know about yourself and how your chart reacts to a variety of situations, the better you can accurately predict the outcome.

Empowered by this self-knowledge, you'll be well prepared to map your future in synch with the planets, your personality, motivations, hopes, wishes, secret desires, and hot buttons. As you start, keep an open mind to the myriad possibilities the planets symbolize. Guard against seeing what you want to see; use predictive astrology to its fullest advantage.

Make predictions, put them in writing, and study your chart after the fact. Doing so will increase your knowledge of predictive astrology and how you and your chart respond to planetary influences. You'll also gain a good understanding of how each planet operates at its best and worst, because each has positives and negatives.

For fun and learning, track the Moon for a month as it moves through the zodiac, contacting your entire natal chart and activating planetary configurations. Keep a diary for future reference.

Astrology is both simple and complex. Work with it, learn from it, and discover why people have relied on it for 4,000 years as an incredible forecasting tool. Make it yours! Map your future!

1
Natal Chart Overview

The natal chart, or birth chart, is the first and foremost tool in predictive astrology. Think of your birth chart as a baseline or foundation that supports your constantly evolving, ever-changing life. You are as unique as each day, and although experiences and events shift your perspective over time, your basic personality remains the same.

Change is an ongoing process that brings what appear to be new viewpoints, directions, and talents as you learn and grow from success and failure alike. Throughout this process, and with the help of the shifting planets, in actuality you are discovering new facets of yourself, previously unrevealed, and untapped strengths and gifts—your hidden potential.

This hidden potential and its flip side—your weaknesses—are found in your natal chart. Through it, you can better map your future, knowing when to act, when to maintain the status quo, and what avenues to pursue to become the best you can be.

An astrological prediction is nothing more than a forecast of how you and your natal chart, which represents you, will respond when presented with a given set of circumstances and planetary alignments.

The natal chart is thus the place to begin. Although a thorough analysis and delineation is preferable, you can easily and quickly capture the essence of the chart by using the method outlined in this chapter. This knowledge, combined with specific predictive techniques, is a good starting point. It gives you a "feel" for your natal chart, how your personality is expressed inwardly and outwardly. These items are included in the overview:

- Hemispheres, quadrants, and houses
- Elements and modes
- Sun and aspects
- Moon and aspects
- Ascendant and aspects
- Angular planets
- Strongest planet(s)

Hemispheres, Quadrants, and Houses

Hemispheres and quadrants can be likened to the big picture, the panoramic view that reveals the first insight into personality. Through them, you can loosely characterize the chart as one belonging to an extrovert or introvert, a people person, or someone who is self-reliant. Although these descriptions are general and stereotypical, they do signify basic lifestyle preferences.

Hemispheres

Count the number of planets in your chart in the northern hemisphere (bottom half) and southern hemisphere (top half) of the chart, which is divided horizontally by the Ascendant/Descendant (first-house cusp/seventh-house cusp) axis, which is also called the horizon (chart 1). Do the same for the western (right) and eastern (left) halves, which are divided vertically by the IC/Midheaven (fourth-house cusp/tenth-house cusp) axis (chart 2).

A balanced distribution of planets, such as a five/five or four/six split between the northern and southern hemispheres or the western and eastern hemispheres, indicates that both influences are operative. An emphasis of planets in one hemisphere or the other, such as a seven/three split, signals a higher comfort level in the hemisphere with the most planets.

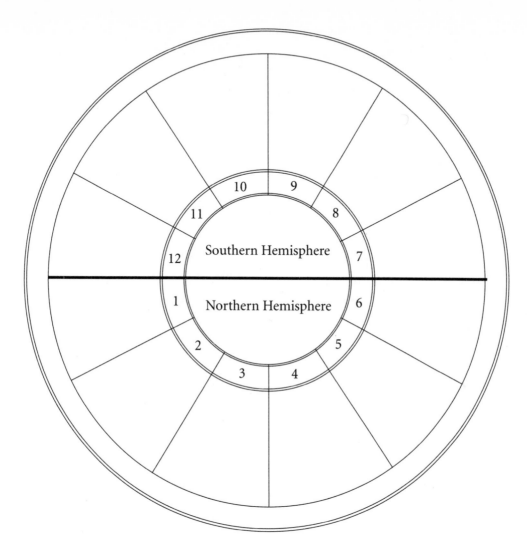

Chart 1
Southern and Northern Hemispheres

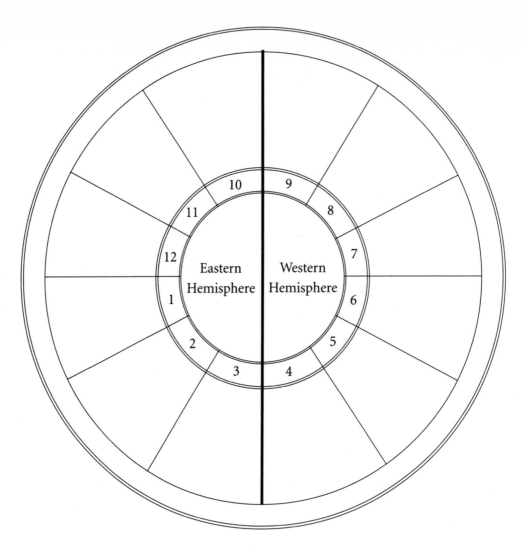

Chart 2
Eastern and Western Hemispheres

- Northern hemisphere—Because this hemisphere is below the horizon, you are introspective and rely on yourself for solutions more often than you consult with others. Generally, but not always, you are more comfortable operating out of the public eye.

- Southern hemisphere—With more planets in this hemisphere, which is above the horizon, you are an extrovert who finds strength in relationships. You ask others for opinions and solutions, and probably have natural leadership ability and enjoy being in public positions.

- Eastern hemisphere—Because the Ascendant, which represents you, is in this hemisphere, your focus is more on your needs and desires. You are self-motivated and action-oriented, and usually go after what you want.

- Western hemisphere—An emphasis on this hemisphere, which includes the Descendant (partners), turns your focus to other people. You are motivated by and responsive to the wants and needs of others.

Quadrants

The quadrants further narrow the focus (chart 3). In many charts, one quadrant is emphasized over the others because the Sun, Mercury, and Venus are never far apart. More commonly, two quadrants contain more planets than the others and therefore represent the dominant energy.

The first quadrant is houses one, two, and three; the second quadrant is houses four, five, and six; the third quadrant is houses seven, eight, and nine; and the fourth quadrant is houses ten, eleven, and twelve.

- First quadrant—This quadrant begins with the Ascendant (you) and combines the influences of the northern and eastern hemispheres. It reinforces independence, and you easily initiate action and express yourself.

- Second quadrant—With the combined influences of the northern and western hemispheres, this quadrant begins with the IC, which represents your roots and family. Although self-directed, you are receptive to others and value their input.

- Third quadrant—Beginning with the Descendant (partners), this quadrant combines the influences of the southern and western hemispheres. Relationships are important to you, and as a people person, you seek advice and opinions.

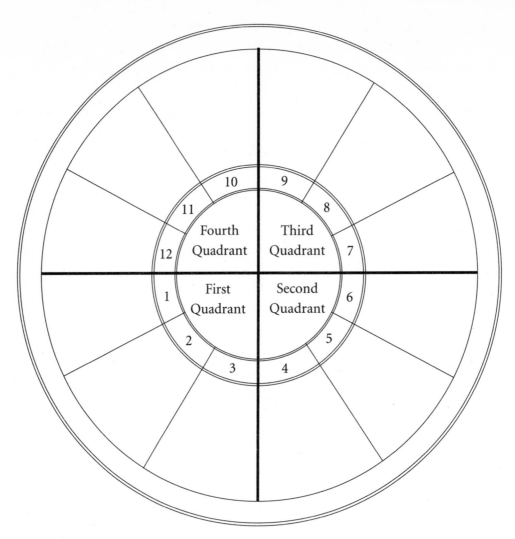

Chart 3
Quadrants

- Fourth quadrant—The fourth quadrant begins with the Midheaven, which is associated with career and status. It combines the influences of the southern and eastern hemispheres. With this emphasis you are self-motivated and ambitious; you value teamwork.

Houses and Angles

A horoscope is divided into twelve pie-shaped pieces called houses (chart 4). Each house is associated with a particular area of life, such as money, health, romance, or career. The dividing lines between houses are called cusps.

House emphasis further narrows the scope of the hemispheres and quadrants. If you have three planets in the first house, for example, and none in the second or third house, personal affairs will benefit from your initiative. With the three planets in the second house, action would center on money matters and self-esteem.

Each house is also associated with a zodiacal ruling sign. Just as the houses are numbered one through twelve, the twelve signs follow in sequence from Aries to Pisces. Chart 4 shows the sign associated with each house.

The houses and their areas of influence are as follows:

- First house—Self, outward expression of personality, personal affairs, vitality, strength, stature, coordination, physical constitution, outlook on life
- Second house—Income, possessions, self-esteem, values, giving, receiving, morals, wealth, spending habits, debt
- Third house—Communication, transportation, short trips, neighbors, siblings, perceptions, contracts, short trips, intellect, early education
- Fourth house—Home, family, parents, father,[1] beginnings and endings, family traditions, land, property, home life
- Fifth house—Romance, children, creativity, recreation, sports, hobbies, love affairs, theaters, gambling, exercise, fun
- Sixth house—Work, service, job, health (minor illnesses), co-workers, employees, pets, diet, food, medical personnel, volunteer activities
- Seventh house—Partners, relationships, marriage, rivals, agreements, divorce, peace, social life, lawsuits, social skills

---

1. Some astrologers associate the mother with the fourth house and the father with the tenth house. Experiment with both to see which works best for your birth chart.

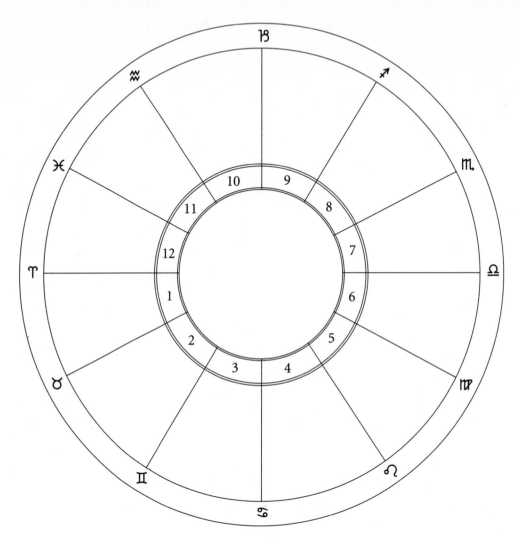

Chart 4
Houses and Signs

- Eighth house—Joint resources, sex, inheritance, insurance, wills, legacies, spousal maintenance, bankruptcy, taxes
- Ninth house—Travel, education, legal affairs, spirituality, judgment, ethics, religion, lawyers, philosophy
- Tenth house—Career, ambition, status, reputation, retirement, supervisors, employers, mother, fame, honors, popularity, prestige, promotion
- Eleventh house—Friends, groups, goals and objectives, hopes and wishes, clubs, organizations, stepchildren, networking
- Twelfth house—Compassion, health (long-term illnesses, hospitalization), secrets, intuition, difficult tasks, self-undoing, secret rivals, introspection, sleep, meditation

The dividing line between one house and another is called a cusp. The first, fourth, seventh and tenth-house cusps are known as angles; each has a special name and is an important and powerful point in the natal chart. (The angles are used extensively in predictive astrology.)

- First-house cusp—Ascendant (you)
- Fourth-house cusp—IC (home and family)
- Seventh-house cusp—Descendant (partnerships)
- Tenth-house cusp—Midheaven (career and status)

Elements and Modes

The four elements—fire, earth, air, and water—define another layer of personality that reflects your basic responses. Each sign is associated with one element, and each planet is in one sign/element (chart 5).

Most people are a combination of all four elements, although one or two usually dominate, in part because the Sun, Mercury, and Venus are always close together. The Ascendant and Midheaven signs sometimes tip the balance to make one element stronger than another.

Occasionally an element is absent, but other factors usually compensate. For example, a chart without any planets in water signs could have one or more planets in water houses—those houses that are naturally associated with the water signs (fourth, eighth, and twelfth houses).

Here are the elements, signs, and glyphs:

Fire	Earth	Air	Water
Aries ♈	Taurus ♉	Gemini ♊	Cancer ♋
Leo ♌	Virgo ♍	Libra ♎	Scorpio ♏
Sagittarius ♐	Capricorn ♑	Aquarius ♒	Pisces ♓

Fire—Action-oriented, enthusiastic, impatient, spontaneous, risk taker

Earth—Practical, linear, efficient, common sense, needs security

Air—Intellectual, logical, communicator, restless, thinks rather than feels

Water—Sensitive, receptive, impractical, compassionate, intuitive

The three modes—cardinal, fixed, and mutable—describe your preferred method of operation. As is true with the elements, each sign is associated with one mode (chart 5) and each planet is in one mode. All three modes are usually present somewhere in your chart, even if only by one or more planets in houses naturally ruled by that mode.

The dominant pattern is revealed in the mode that contains the most planets. As with the elements, the Ascendant and Midheaven signs are counted along with the planets.

Here are the modes, signs, and glyphs:

Cardinal	Fixed	Mutable
Aries ♈	Taurus ♉	Gemini ♊
Cancer ♋	Leo ♌	Virgo ♍
Libra ♎	Scorpio ♏	Sagittarius ♐
Capricorn ♑	Aquarius ♒	Pisces ♓

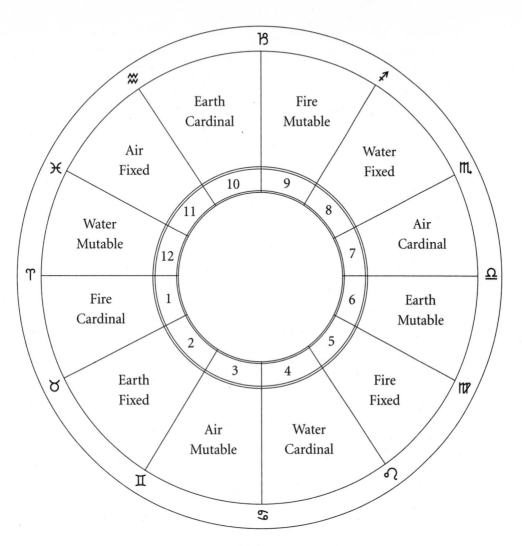

Chart 5
Elements and Modes

Cardinal—Enjoys challenges, initiates, likes change, persistent

Fixed—Determined, stubborn, dislikes change, follow-through

Mutable—Flexible, easygoing, procrastinates, indecisive

Each sign is a combination of one element and one mode. Together, they signify the basic energy of the sign:

Aries—cardinal fire   Taurus—fixed earth

Gemini—mutable air   Cancer—cardinal water

Leo—fixed fire   Virgo—mutable earth

Libra—cardinal air   Scorpio—fixed water

Sagittarius—mutable fire Capricorn—cardinal earth

Aquarius—fixed air   Pisces—mutable water

With the elements and modes combined, the following keyword traits are representative of the signs:

- Aries—Initiative, energy, headstrong, impatient, enthusiastic, ambitious, insomnia, physical activity, anger, courage, pioneer
- Taurus—Secure, stable, placid, materialistic, determined, passive, stubborn, jealous, rigid, lazy, artistic, conservative, devoted
- Gemini—Adaptable, sociable, flirtatious, versatile, talkative, nervous, restless, alert, active, impatient, scattered, studious
- Cancer—Tied to the past, emotional, domestic, self-indulgent, touchy, intuitive, moody, cautious, patriotic, nurturing, impressionable
- Leo—Confident, vital, leadership, dynamic, ambitious, snobbish, selfish, vain, loyal, honorable, determined, affectionate, generous
- Virgo—Practical, honest, analytical, meticulous, critical, worrisome, precise, detail-oriented, reserved, dependable, discriminating, nervous
- Libra—Partnership, idealistic, refined, cooperative, impatient, vain, dependent, indecisive, considerate, neat, appreciative, balanced
- Scorpio—Magnetic, secretive, competitive, jealous, stubborn, domineering, tenacious, creative, emotional, penetrating, distrustful

- Sagittarius—Philosophical, restless, optimistic, self-righteous, indulgent, spendthrift, generous, open-minded, honest, inspirational

- Capricorn—Conservative, ambitious, responsible, selfish, rigid, pessimistic, stingy, trustworthy, dependable, industrious, patient

- Aquarius—Independent, intellectual, freedom-loving, eccentric, rebellious, faddish, cold, intuitive, persevering, inventive

- Pisces—Receptive, sensitive, impressionable, spiritual, indulgent, moody, impractical, hypersensitive, sympathetic, giving

Planets, Ascendant, and Aspects

There are ten planets in a horoscope—the Sun, Moon, Mercury, Venus, Mars, Jupiter, Saturn, Uranus, Neptune, and Pluto. (The Sun and Moon are referred to as planets for ease in terminology.) Each is associated with certain characteristics in predictive astrology, which are explained in succeeding chapters. To keep things simple, only the Sun, Moon, and Ascendant are included in the natal chart overview. However, the other planets and the Midheaven (tenth-house cusp, career point) are included in this section because it's helpful in both natal and predictive astrology to have a basic understanding of them and how they function in the signs. Here are the planets and their glyphs and keywords:

- Sun ☉—Strength, individuality, honor, willpower, arrogance, willfulness, dictatorial, loyalty, confidence, leadership

- Moon ☽—Nurturing, changeable, inspirational, moody, possessive, materialistic, romantic, flexible, sociable, receptive, domestic

- Mercury ☿—Intellectual, observant, efficient, nervous, critical, articulate, adaptable, unstable, worrisome, skeptical, expressive

- Venus ♀—Beauty, cooperation, harmonious, love, charm, frivolous, overly sensitive, vain, indolent, gentle, appreciative

- Mars ♂—Energetic, independent, courageous, aggressive, combative, jealous, coarse, defiant, self-reliant, enthusiastic, active

- Jupiter ♃—Generous, fortunate, faithful, idealistic, impractical, gullible, fanatical, extravagant, tolerant, confident, popular

- Saturn ♄—Responsible, serious, thrifty, patient, severe, pessimistic, rigid, selfish, wise, stable, sincere, humble, enduring, punctual
- Uranus ♅—Independent, friendly, impulsive, eccentric, rebellious, fanatical, erratic, unbiased, magnetic, strong-willed, humanitarian
- Neptune ♆—Idealistic, psychic, inspirational, sympathetic, fearful, deceptive, self-indulgent, compassionate, creative, spiritual
- Pluto ♇—Transformation, occult, reckless, destructive, rejuvenation, regeneration, intense, spiritual, psychic, nonconforming

Sun

The Sun represents the life force, your inner self and basic drive. It is your primary motivator, why you get out of bed in the morning, your reason for being. As one of the two most important planets in your chart (along with the Moon), the Sun defines you and your core desires, interests, and psychological make-up.

However, solar energy rarely shows itself in its purest form because other planets can modify it. A person who has the Sun and Uranus near each other in the birth chart, for example, will display Aquarius characteristics because Uranus is the planet associated with Aquarius. Depending on the compatibility of the specific planetary energies, this can be a positive or negative force.

Aries Sun—Impulsive, self-starter, initiator, impatient

Taurus Sun—Practical, stubborn, possessive, sensual

Gemini Sun—Communicative, social, curious, changeable

Cancer Sun—Nurturing, protective, emotional, clingy

Leo Sun—Generous, proud, showy, stubborn

Virgo Sun—Observant, particular, logical, practical

Libra Sun—Diplomatic, indecisive, companionable, cooperative

Scorpio Sun—Deep, passionate, tenacious, vengeful

Sagittarius Sun—Optimistic, idealistic, uninhibited, expansive

Capricorn Sun—Ambitious, practical, cautious, controlled

Aquarius Sun—Independent, humanitarian, stubborn, intellectual

Pisces Sun—Emotional, compassionate, self-sacrificing, absent-minded

Moon

The Moon rules emotions, sensitivities, and moods. It also expresses its energy as habitual behavior, automatic responses, and subconscious reactions. As a personality component, the Moon's sign shows how you respond to feelings triggered by others or generated by your own psyche. Like the Sun (and the other planets), the Moon's basic energy is modified through contacts with other planets.

Aries Moon—Spirited, ardent, quick response

Taurus Moon—Sensual, needs routine and stability

Gemini Moon—Mental orientation, thinks through feelings

Cancer Moon—Intuitive, nurturing, supportive

Leo Moon—Needs attention and praise, generous

Virgo Moon—Analyzes feelings, worrier

Libra Moon—Needs peace, harmony, contact with others

Scorpio Moon—Possessive, intense, deep feelings

Sagittarius Moon—Blunt response, needs adventure

Capricorn Moon—Practical, ambitious, distant

Aquarius Moon—Thinks more than feels, fond of friends, intuitive

Pisces Moon—Sensitive, deep emotions, needs quiet time

Ascendant

The Ascendant, or rising sign, represents the face you show to the world. It is your outer personality, the side of you most people see. In contrast to the Sun, which represents your inner motivations, the Ascendant acts as a filter through which you view the world. Other planets can influence or modify the Ascendant, just as they do when one planet is linked to another planet.

Aries Ascendant—Assertive, spontaneous, fiery

Taurus Ascendant—Reliable, thorough, stable, practical

Gemini Ascendant—Curious, communicative, scattered

Cancer Ascendant—Protective, sensitive, easily hurt

Leo Ascendant—Warm, outgoing, generous, creative

Virgo Ascendant—Precise, discriminating, perfectionist

Libra Ascendant—Fair, seeks balance, considerate of others

Scorpio Ascendant—Intense, poker face, relentless

Sagittarius Ascendant—Enthusiastic, adventuresome, skips details

Capricorn Ascendant—Status-oriented, reserved, responsible

Aquarius Ascendant—Objective, intellectual, unconventional, detached

Pisces Ascendant—Compassionate, inspirational, self-sacrificing

Mercury

Mercury rules your thinking process, how you make decisions, and your overall communication style. Because it always travels near the Sun, Mercury is usually in the Sun sign or the sign before or after it, depending on Mercury's speed.

Mercury turns retrograde for two to three weeks, three or four times each year. When retrograde, it appears to move in reverse motion, thus retreating to the sign before the Sun sign. A natal retrograde Mercury is intuitive, introspective, subjective, and hesitant to express ideas. When stationary (the point at which it appears to stop before turning retrograde or direct), Mercury's characteristics in the sign it occupies are intensified.

Aries Mercury—Quick thinking, argumentative, decisive, impulsive

Taurus Mercury—Common sense, concentration, practical, stubborn

Gemini Mercury—Inventive, logical, curious, scattered

Cancer Mercury—Emotional thinking, good memory, sensitive, subjective

Leo Mercury—Creative, dramatic, opinionated, arrogant

Virgo Mercury—Logical, analytical, reticent, detail-oriented

Libra Mercury—Impartial, indecisive, honest, persuasive

Scorpio Mercury—Intuitive, secretive, sarcastic, determined

Sagittarius Mercury—Idealistic, well informed, blunt, truthful

Capricorn Mercury—Methodical, ambitious, organized, stern

Aquarius Mercury—Inventive, intuitive, objective, stubborn

Pisces Mercury—Imaginative, intuitive, sympathetic, sensitive

Venus

Venus rules attraction, social interaction, affection, love and marriage, and business partnerships. It's also the universal planet of money, income, and possessions.

Like Mercury, Venus travels close to the Sun, turning retrograde about every eighteen months, for about six weeks at a time. People born with Venus retrograde are less social than those who have Venus direct and slower to develop financial security. A stationary Venus has the opposite effect, strengthening the planet's influence.

Aries Venus—Passionate, aggressive, self-centered, ardent

Taurus Venus—Steadfast, loyal, possessive, sensual

Gemini Venus—Flirtatious, freedom-loving, social, fickle

Cancer Venus—Security, affection, sentimental, moody

Leo Venus—Ardent, extravagant, snobbish, romantic

Virgo Venus—Choosy, thrifty, critical, shy

Libra Venus—Harmonious, refined, well liked, status-seeking

Scorpio Venus—Passionate, jealous, shrewd, manipulative

Sagittarius Venus—Sociable, easygoing, open, dogmatic

Capricorn Venus—Loyal, status-seeking, unemotional, responsible

Aquarius Venus—Generous, freedom-loving, impersonal, eccentric

Pisces Venus—Romantic, impractical, compassionate, dependent

Mars

The action planet Mars represents energy and drive, initiative and challenge. Its negative influence becomes apparent when expressed as anger and resentment. Mars reflects your stamina, the desires that motivate you, and where and how you direct your ambitions.

If you were born when Mars was retrograde (a six-month period about every two years), you generally work harder than others and must consciously direct your energy outward rather than inward. A stationary Mars manifests as concentrated energy, adding extra drive.

Aries Mars—Initiative, courageous, competitive, headstrong

Taurus Mars—Determined, persevering, jealousy, slow to act

Gemini Mars—Restless, impetuous, active, argumentative

Cancer Mars—Subjective, emotional, resentful, ardent

Leo Mars—Leadership, determined, ambitious, egotistical

Virgo Mars—Efficient, fastidious, systematic, fussy

Libra Mars—Fair, social, indecisive, compromising

Scorpio Mars—Drive, willpower, resentment, courageous

Sagittarius Mars—Adventurous, crusader, direct, self-righteous

Capricorn Mars—Ambitious, organized, materialistic, disciplined

Aquarius Mars—Independent, innovative, revolutionary, team player

Pisces Mars—Resentful, indecisive, charitable, emotional

Jupiter

Associated with luck, expansion, opportunities, and overall abundance, Jupiter can also represent too much of a good thing. Used positively, Jupiter can add to your life success potential; used negatively, it can amplify less desirable characteristics.

Jupiter also governs religion, spirituality, morals, and ethics. Where Mercury represents practical, everyday decisions and thoughts, Jupiter thinking is big-picture and abstract. It helps you see the possibilities beyond the obvious.

Aries Jupiter—Generous, extravagant, leadership, self-importance

Taurus Jupiter—Resourceful, self-indulgent, wealthy, materialistic

Gemini Jupiter—Knowledgeable, clever, restless, communicator

Cancer Jupiter—Benevolent, kind, nurturing, overeater

Leo Jupiter—Self-important, generous, enthusiastic, self-confident

Virgo Jupiter—Moralistic, observant, service-oriented, honest

Libra Jupiter—Self-sacrificing, well liked, diplomatic, false promises

Scorpio Jupiter—Principled, willpower, uncompromising, secretive

Sagittarius Jupiter—Truth seeker, lucky, multicultural, narrow-minded

Capricorn Jupiter—Economical, ethical, cautious, power seeker

Aquarius Jupiter—Humanitarian, impartial, tolerant, unrealistic

Pisces Jupiter—Self-sacrificing, compassionate, spiritual, undisciplined

Saturn

With Saturn comes responsibility, hard work, reality, delays, and discouragement. But Saturn also delivers rewards if you follow its rules, as well as learning experiences, both positive and negative. In essence, Saturn challenges you to establish a firm foundation on which to build future successes. It is the universal business planet.

Often called the karmic planet, Saturn is a constant reminder of the past, teaching through experience. If you have a strong Saturn in your natal chart (see "Dominant Planets" later in this chapter), you may more often than not experience "instant karma"; that is, an almost instantaneous reaction to an action initiated by you.

Aries Saturn—Enterprising, impatient, self-reliant, defensive

Taurus Saturn—Sensible, patient, stable, obstinate

Gemini Saturn—Logical, practical, undisciplined, systematic

Cancer Saturn—Tenacious, emotional restrain, dignified, responsible

Leo Saturn—Self-centered, leadership, rigid, recognition

Virgo Saturn—Methodical, exacting, hard-working, worrisome

Libra Saturn—Uncooperative, committed, karmic relationships, tactful

Scorpio Saturn—Calculating, intense, responsible, diligent

Sagittarius Saturn—Moralistic, rigid, diligent, leadership

Capricorn Saturn—Ambitious, stingy, hard-working, security

Aquarius Saturn—Impartial, unconventional, concentration, cold

Pisces Saturn—Humility, meditation, solitude, regret

Uranus

Uranus represents change, the unexpected, disruption, innovation, rebellion, and all things labeled "unconventional." It's also the planet of the humanitarian, identifying strongly with personal freedoms and the concept that people have the right to choose their own destiny. Uranus is also associated with intuition, flashes of insight, and sudden understanding.

As an outer planet (Jupiter, Saturn, Uranus, Neptune, and Pluto are called "outer planets" because they are the farthest from the Sun), Uranus influences worldwide trends in addition to the personal characteristics reflected in the natal chart. For example, the

Internet came of age when Uranus was in Aquarius, the sign it rules (see "Planetary Rulerships" later in this chapter).

Aries Uranus—Tempestuous, independent, trailblazer, impulsive

Taurus Uranus—Practical innovation, stubborn, artistic, humanitarian

Gemini Uranus—Erratic, ingenious, intuitive, traveler

Cancer Uranus—Lifestyle freedom, intuitive, moody, unusual family

Leo Uranus—Leadership, creativity, stubborn, compromising

Virgo Uranus—Healing, systematic, practical, hard worker

Libra Uranus—Relationship freedom, intuitive, justice, groups

Scorpio Uranus—Rebellious, resourceful, intense emotions, decisive

Sagittarius Uranus—Intellectual freedom, traveler, multicultural, pioneer

Capricorn Uranus—Practical change, success, ambitious, insecurity

Aquarius Uranus—Humanitarian, innovative, inventive, independent

Pisces Uranus—Intuitive, idealistic, spiritual, subconscious

Neptune

The diverse energy of Neptune rules creative and artistic genius as well as self-delusion, addiction, and escapism. It can spark your imagination or send you in search of a rainbow as reality competes with fantasy.

At its best, Neptune represents spirituality, vision, and compassion. It also governs the psychic realm, giving some people the ability to transcend the Earth plane to sense, hear, or see what others cannot. Neptune is involved in hunches and intuitive impressions.

Aries Neptune—Imaginative, intuitive, egotistical

Taurus Neptune—Materialistic, practical, artistic

Gemini Neptune—Intuitive, imaginative, superficial

Cancer Neptune—Psychic, sentimental, sensitive

Leo Neptune—Creative, extravagant, impractical

Virgo Neptune—Self-doubt, practical imagination, materialism

Libra Neptune—Social responsibility, idealistic love, creativity

Scorpio Neptune—Emotional intensity, intuitive, moral

Sagittarius Neptune—Values, spirituality, meditation

Capricorn Neptune—Ethics, dissolution, economic change

Aquarius Neptune—Intuition, tolerance, philanthropy

Pisces Neptune—Music, creative, psychic

Pluto

Known as the planet of transformation and regeneration, Pluto is identified with massive change, purging what is old and worn to begin anew. Plutonian energy is powerful and unrelenting. As with the other outer planets, Pluto reflects broad societal changes, such as consumer recycling, layoffs, and unemployment.

Pluto's influence in the natal chart is sometimes strong, sometimes weaker, depending upon the aspects it makes to other birth-chart planets. Pluto is strong in the birth chart, for example, when trine the Sun; but if Pluto's only aspect is a conjunction to Neptune, it is more a generational influence than a personal one. It is associated with areas of loss as well as life-changing personal events, which are often ultimately viewed as positive.

As the ruler of Scorpio, Pluto rules other people's money, such as inheritance, insurance, and loans.

Aries Pluto—Pioneer, self-reliant

Taurus Pluto—Materialistic, traditional

Gemini Pluto—Inventive, technology

Cancer Pluto—Family, economics

Leo Pluto—Power struggle, ego

Virgo Pluto—Health, employment

Libra Pluto—Justice, diplomacy

Scorpio Pluto—Regeneration, economics

Sagittarius Pluto—Spirituality, law

Capricorn Pluto—Economics, government

Aquarius Pluto—Revolution, freedom

Pisces Pluto—Creative, psychic

Midheaven

Like the Ascendant, the Midheaven is an important and sensitive point in the chart. It represents status, career, and reputation. The natal sign on your Midheaven indicates potential career areas, your approach to your career, and what you hope to gain from it.

Aries Midheaven—Ambitious, entrepreneurial, leadership, impatient

Taurus Midheaven—Financial gain, stability, persistence, tolerance

Gemini Midheaven—Diversity, communication, multitasking, instability

Cancer Midheaven—Independence, security, self-employment, defensive

Leo Midheaven—Authority, ego, leadership, impatient

Virgo Midheaven—Purposeful, practical, security, overly sensitive

Libra Midheaven—Tact, public image, cooperation, insincerity

Scorpio Midheaven—Determined, goal-oriented, ambitious, ruthless

Sagittarius Midheaven—Idealistic, virtuous, future-oriented, optimistic

Capricorn Midheaven—Ambitious, hard-working, responsible, slow climb

Aquarius Midheaven—Teamwork, efficient, innovative, independent

Pisces Midheaven—Solitude, tranquility, empathy, passivity

Aspects

An aspect is a geometric angle that links the energy of two or more planets (chart 6). It modifies, or colors, the planets involved to reflect a dual influence. Mercury and Neptune connected by a trine aspect, for example, add charm and creativity, while the same two planets in square aspect can indicate deception.

Orbs are used to determine which planets are in aspect. Although a conjunction is defined as two planets in the same sign at the same degree, the aspect is effective with an orb of up to eight degrees. This means that two planets at 10° Aries are conjunct, and also that two planets five degrees apart—the first at 10° Aries and the second at 15° Aries—also form a conjunction. A trine connects two planets that are 120 degrees apart, such as one at 12° Gemini and another at 16° Aquarius.

The major aspects and their glyphs, degrees, orbs, and basic meanings are listed here. These are not the only aspects used by astrologers, but they are the easiest to identify and also those that have the strongest influence. The orbs mentioned here are for natal charts. Much narrower orbs are used in predictive astrology, as is explained in chapter 2.

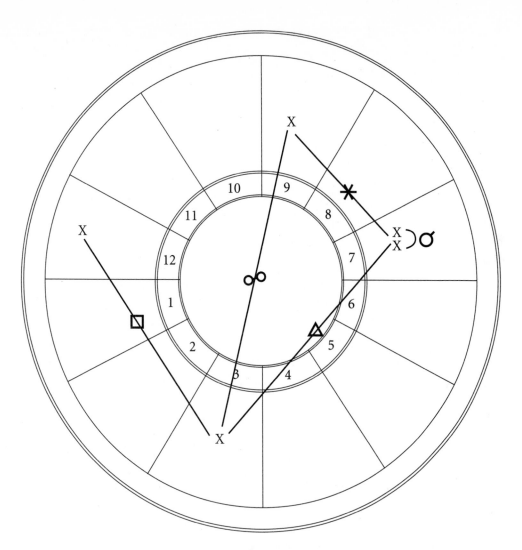

Chart 6
Aspects

Aspect	Glyph	Degrees	Orb	Significance
Conjunction	☌	0 degrees	8 degrees	Intensity
Trine	△	120 degrees	8 degrees	Ease, luck
Sextile	✶	60 degrees	6 degrees	Opportunity
Square	□	90 degrees	8 degrees	Conflict, action
Opposition	☍	180 degrees	8 degrees	Separation

Two minor aspects—the semisquare (∠) and sesquisquare (⌑)—are especially useful in predictive astrology. Similar to the square, they also signify action and conflict. These aspects are also valid for natal chart interpretation.

Planetary Rulerships

Each sign is associated with, or ruled by, a planet, such as Aries and Mars. A planet is most comfortable when in the sign it rules, where it can most freely express its energy. The planet ruling the sign on a house cusp is said to rule that house.

   The following list includes the modern and ancient rulers for Scorpio, Aquarius, and Pisces. The second planet listed was the designated ruler prior to the discovery of Uranus, Neptune, and Pluto. Both are effective in predictive astrology.

Aries—Mars	Leo—Sun	Sagittarius—Jupiter
Taurus—Venus	Virgo—Mercury	Capricorn—Saturn
Gemini—Mercury	Libra—Venus	Aquarius—Uranus, Saturn
Cancer—Moon	Scorpio—Pluto, Mars	Pisces—Neptune, Jupiter

Dominant Planets

Planets in the first house within five degrees of the Ascendant (called a rising planet) color the personality, in some cases almost overpowering the basic nature of the rising sign. More than a blending of the two energies, the rising planet either intensifies the sign or gives the personality strong characteristics of the sign the planet naturally rules.

   If you have Saturn rising, for example, you function much as a Capricorn would, but within the context of the rising sign. Saturn in Aries would tone down the impulsive nature of that sign, while Saturn in Capricorn would strengthen the Capricorn energy.

Rising planets also characterize the personality to the point that they take on a major role in determining basic responses, interests, general day-to-day routines, and dominant areas of life. Mercury rising emphasizes the importance of communication, Venus does the same with relationships, and Neptune gives the ability to adapt, to fit into any situation.

It's also important to identify other strong planet(s) in the chart, beyond those conjunct the Ascendant. They too play a prominent role in shaping the personality and life events. Although "strength" is a judgment call, these guidelines are helpful and a good place to begin:

- Angular planets—Those in the first, fourth, seventh, and tenth houses. The closer they are to the angle (house cusp), the stronger they are.

- Planets in aspect to angular planets—Their energy is channeled to the angular house.

- Aspects—The narrower the orb, the stronger the aspect and, therefore, the planets involved.

- Mutual reception—Two planets in aspect and in each other's signs (for example, the Sun in Capricorn trine Saturn in Leo—the Sun is the natural ruler of Leo, and Saturn is the natural ruler of Capricorn).

- Planets in their ruling sign—For example, Mercury in Gemini, Jupiter in Sagittarius.

- Major configurations—planets in a grand trine, t-square, stellium, or grand square—tend to be a dominant factor in an individual's life, but are not always the strongest planets in the chart. This is more likely if the configuration is angular or involves the Sun and Moon. In a grand trine, three planets form a triangle shape; each leg of the triangle is 120 degrees. A t-square is two planets in opposition and both of them square a third, forming a "T". Three planets conjunct each other is a stellium. A grand square is two oppositions that cross each other, forming four squares. The number of planets mentioned for each configuration is the minimum; they often have more, such as a conjunction of two planets in opposition to one.

- Ascendant and Midheaven rulers—If other indicators suggest these planets are strong, they get an extra "boost" from their rulership status. The ruler of the Ascendant, Midheaven, or house is the planet associated with the sign on the Ascendant, Midheaven, or house cusp. Where intercepted signs (those that are wholly contained within a house and not on a house cusp) occur, the house has co-rulers— two signs and their ruling planets influence the affairs of the house.

2
Predictive Techniques

There are many techniques available to the predictive astrologer. Only the traditional ones are included in this book. Once you've mastered them, you can move on to more advanced methods.

These basic techniques, followed step by step, reveal a complete picture of forthcoming trends and events. Predictive astrology is a four-step process:

- Natal chart overview
- Secondary progressions
- Outer planet transits and eclipses
- Inner planet transits and new and full Moons

Imagine a pyramid. It sits on a wide base that gradually tapers to a point. The base is the natal chart, with each successive technique building on the last, progressively narrowing from overall trends to the specific timing of events (chart 7).

Secondary progressions are trendsetters. They indicate the major background themes in effect for approximately a year. Outer planet (Jupiter, Saturn, Uranus, Neptune, and Pluto) transits further refine and narrow the picture and set up the potential for events, as do eclipses. New and full Moons and the inner transiting planets function as timers and triggers; they indicate when an event is likely to occur.

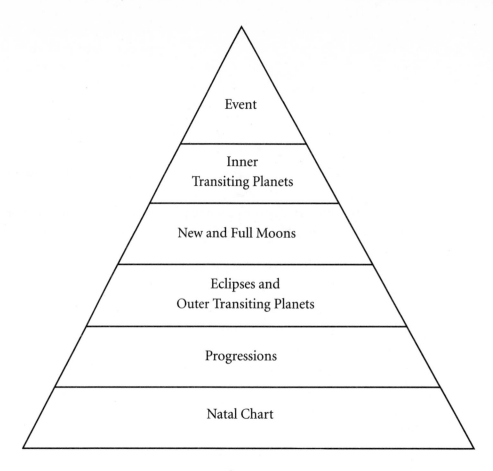

Chart 7
Predictive Techniques

You'll have much success in predicting events using this basic method. All it takes is practice, persistence, and experience. Begin with your chart—you know yourself best and therefore can learn most easily by predicting personal events and tracking the outcome. The charts of close friends and relatives (who will give you feedback) are also good learning material.

Secondary Progressions

Secondary progressions, commonly referred to as secondaries or progressions, use the day-for-a-year method of planetary movement. They are based on the actual daily movement of the planets, with each day corresponding to a year. For example, to determine the progressed influences in effect when you were age ten, count forward ten days in an ephemeris (a listing of the sign, degrees, and minutes of each planet on a daily basis), beginning with the day after your birthday (month, day, year). The planets at age ten for a May 20 birth would be those listed for May 30 of the same year. A September 6 birth date would be September 16, and so on.

Each planet has an average annual motion, but the only one that maintains this constant is the Sun, and the Sun and Moon never turn retrograde, as do the other planets. The progressed Sun moves approximately one degree for every year of life. The Moon's daily motion varies, depending on the sign it is in, but the progressed Moon returns to its natal place about every twenty-eight years.

When planets turn retrograde, they appear to move backward in the heavens. The ephemeris shows the degrees and minutes decreasing instead of increasing. Planets slow their speed as they approach retrograde and direct stations. A station is the point at which a planet appears to stop before changing direction, either backward or forward.

Pluto can remain at the same degree for ten to fifteen days, which equates to ten to fifteen years by progression. Saturn can do the same for five days/years, Mars for two or three days/years, and Mercury for one day/year.

Venus moves more than one degree a day (one degree a year by progression) at its fastest, gradually slowing to a one- to two-day (one to two years by progression) stationary period as it prepares to reverse direction. Depending on the birth date, Venus usually progresses through one to three signs in a lifetime. Because of its overall faster motion, progressed Mercury usually travels through two, three, or four signs. Retrograde periods cause the variation.

Progressed Jupiter sometimes changes signs in progression, but the other outer planets—Saturn, Uranus, Neptune, and Pluto—must be in the last degrees of a sign to change signs because their movement is so slow. The outer planets sometimes progress no more than a degree or two in a lifetime.

Here is the average annual movement of progressed planets:

Sun—1 degree   Moon—12 degrees

Mercury—1 degree, 23 minutes   Venus—1 degree, 12 minutes

Mars—31 minutes   Jupiter—5 minutes

Saturn—2 minutes   Uranus—42 seconds

Neptune—24 seconds   Pluto—1 second

The Sun, Moon, Mercury, Venus, Mars, and sometimes Jupiter can move fast enough in a lifetime to perfect (make exact) natal aspects. That is, the first of two planets in a natal aspect could progress forward, narrowing the gap until it reaches the exact same degree as the second planet.

Progressed planets form aspects with natal planets and other progressed planets. These contacts are important indicators in predictive astrology.

The progressed outer planets Saturn, Uranus, Neptune, and Pluto move so slowly that they rarely form aspects not present at birth. If a natal aspect involving an outer planet is nearly exact, the planet could progress forward and close the gap, thereby eliminating the orb. But this in itself is unlikely to manifest as an event unless triggered by a faster-moving transiting planet. The exact aspect then presents the opportunity to fully realize one's natal potential.

Progressed Sign and House Changes

Although natal characteristics always dominate, their energy is modified when a progressed planet enters another sign. The effect is that of adding or opening up another layer of resources to explore and tap. For example, family and security are major areas of interest if you have Mars in Cancer. This will be true throughout your lifetime. But if Mars progresses into Leo, personal needs will become a higher priority than in previous years.

These energy shifts are more easily felt with the faster-moving progressed Moon, which changes sign about every two-and-a-half years.

A similar effect occurs when a planet enters another house. If you have natal Venus in the seventh house, relationships will be prominent throughout your life. When Venus progresses into the eighth house, you could form a business/financial partnership or otherwise learn to meld your resources with those of others. Or, if you have a twelfth-house natal Sun, your self-confidence will rise when the Sun progresses into your first house.

Retrograde and Stationary Progressed Planets

The easiest way to spot the years when progressed planets station to turn retrograde or direct is to look at an ephemeris. Count forward in the ephemeris for two to three months, beginning with the day after your birth (remember, one day equals one year), and note the age at which a planet turns retrograde (℞) or direct (D). A year in which a progressed planet reverses direction signals a major turning point. The effect is usually immediately apparent (within a few months) when Venus, Mercury, or Mars changes direction; it's more subtle with the outer planets, and you may not realize the full impact until several years later. (An ephemeris is also the easiest way to discover whether you were born on a day when a planet reversed its direction.)

Higher education, for example, might be delayed if you have a natal retrograde Mercury-Saturn opposition in the ninth/third houses. In the year that progressed Mercury turns direct, you could have a sudden urge to enroll in college. That decision will have a career impact when progressed Mercury later conjoins your Midheaven.

Venus or a seventh-house planet changing direction brings relationships into focus, often resulting in marriage or divorce. A tenth-house planet can indicate a shift in career direction, and a second-house or eighth-house planet can affect finances. House rulerships also provide clues to the outcome. Mars turning direct in a chart with Aries rising acts as a confidence builder.

Retrograde progressed planets manifest in yet another way that might or might not release the promised potential of the natal chart. This occurs when a faster-moving retrograde planet (usually Mercury, Venus, Mars, or Jupiter) precedes by degree a planet it aspects.

For example, one possible outcome of a natal Jupiter-Pluto trine is a sizable inheritance. But suppose that, at birth, Pluto is at sixteen degrees, and Venus is retrograde at fourteen degrees. The natal promise of an inheritance would most likely occur during the year(s) that progressed Venus is exactly trine natal Pluto. This could be one year or sixty or more, depending on how long it takes Venus to retrograde into its station, resume forward movement, and move past its natal position to form the exact aspect with Pluto. For people born during the stationary or early retrograde period, it may never reach exactitude.

Ascendant and Midheaven

The progressed Ascendant and Midheaven, also referred to as angles, are highly significant in predictive astrology. Their opposing points, the IC and Descendant (the other two angles), are, of course, simultaneously aspected.

As in the natal chart, the progressed Ascendant is a personality factor, and the progressed Midheaven governs career, status, and achievements. Although they, like the progressed planets, reflect trends and potential events, their influence is weaker than that of the natal angles.

A progressed planet aspecting the natal Ascendant or Midheaven signals a major event 99 percent of the time. The event usually focuses on the self (Ascendant), partners (Descendant), career (Midheaven), and home/family (IC).

Progressed Aspects and Orbs

The major progressed aspects are easy to spot, but they seldom tell the full story. Although more difficult to see at a glance, the semisquare (45°) and sesquisquare (135°) are similar to the square and often signal potential events. If math isn't your strong suit, purchase an aspectarian to help you find the 45° and 135° aspects. Or use an astrological software program to run a "hit list" of progressed aspects for two to three years so you can spot upcoming trends.

Generally, progressed aspects to natal and progressed planets react like this:

- Conjunction—Intensity, action, joins the forces of two planets
- Trine—Rarely an action aspect, it provides luck and harmony
- Sextile—Creates opportunities, but requires action to realize gain
- Opposition—Usually involves relationships, people at odds, separation
- Square—Action, conflict, matters requiring attention
- Semisquare and sesquisquare—Action, conflict, need for resolution

Usually you will see a combination of background aspects (sextile, trine) and action aspects (conjunction, opposition, square, semisquare, sesquisquare) because the latter are necessary to prompt an event. Action aspects often function this way rather than manifesting as negative events. It is important to look at the overall picture and the planets involved, as well as the natal or progressed energy they're activating.

Effective orbs vary according to the progressed planet, based on the planet's speed of movement:

- Sun—1 degree
- Moon—1½ degrees
- Mercury—1 degree
- Venus—1 degree
- Mars—30 minutes
- Jupiter—15 minutes
- Other outer planets—5 minutes

These recommended orbs are guidelines. Be flexible, and look for both approaching and separating aspects. An approaching aspect is one that has yet to become exact. When two planets are separating, one is moving away from the other after having formed an exact aspect. Faster-moving planets approach and separate from slower-moving ones.

Outer Planet Transits

The term "transit" refers to the movement of the planets through the signs of the horoscope. Your birth chart, for example, shows the position of the transiting planets on the date and at the place and time you were born. From that moment on, the planets have continued to move forward through the signs and houses of your horoscope, some at a rapid rate and others very slowly. As they move, they aspect every planet and angle in your chart. The slowest-moving planets are classified as outer planet transits, while those that move more quickly are called inner planet transits.

The outer planets—Jupiter, Saturn, Neptune, Uranus, and Pluto—function much like progressed planets because of their slow movement. Jupiter is the fastest, transiting one sign about every twelve months, and Pluto is the slowest, moving two or three degrees every year.

These planets, particularly Saturn through Pluto, indicate major life events, usually of long duration. Much of this is the effect of their retrograde pattern as they move forward, station, turn retrograde, station, and resume forward movement. The stationary periods, which can last a month or more with a one-degree approaching and separating orb, have the most impact. Make special note of them.

Three contacts with a natal or progressed planet or angle are usual, although at times they make only two contacts because one of them is a retrograde or direct station. The usual outcome of this cycle is that the first contact brings the issue to your attention, the second contact prompts you to initiate action or signals further developments, and the third contact concludes the matter.

Note: The event or life issue is active as long as the transiting planet will return to within one degree of the natal or progressed planet or angle. The matter might recede into the background—drop lower on your action list—but is nevertheless an ongoing part of your life.

Use a one-degree approaching and separating orb for the outer transiting planets, such as from 10° Gemini to 12° Gemini for a planet at 11° Gemini. But be flexible, especially with retrograde and direct stations. They have more "punch" and often work with a slightly wider orb, and many events occur within a few days or weeks of a station.

The average time it takes for an outer planet to transit a sign is as follows:

- Jupiter—1 year
- Saturn—2½ years
- Uranus—7 years
- Neptune—14 years
- Pluto—21 years

New Moons, Full Moons, Eclipses

New and full Moons occur approximately every twenty-eight days, or about once a month, two weeks apart. In some years, there are thirteen instead of twelve new or full Moons, with two in the same month.

Essentially, new Moons initiate events that culminate at the full Moon. Their contact with a natal or progressed planet or angle activates that energy, bringing it to your attention. Always use narrow orbs, no more than three degrees. The major action aspects—conjunction, square, and opposition—are the strongest.

New and full Moons often activate trends established by the progressed and outer transiting planets. This sometimes happens a day or two before the new or full Moon. On their own and forming no aspects, new and full Moons stimulate matters governed by the house in which they occur, such as communication with the third house or home life with the fourth house.

Eclipses, which are also new or full Moons, have more impact and a longer-lasting effect. Their influence lasts from six to twelve months. Eclipses (four to six per year) are particularly useful in predictive astrology when they echo major trends. An eclipse at a critical point in the chart, such as a progressed planet conjunct a natal one, is an added clue that a long-term event or development is in process.

Inner Planet Transits

The transiting inner planets primarily act as triggers to set off aspects made by progressed and outer transiting planets. They are used to identify the "when" in predictive astrology, and also indicate intermediate steps and the final outcome of major events.

Mars, being the premier action planet, is particularly useful in narrowing the event search to a few days or a week. The Sun, Mercury, and Venus add their energy as well and further identify potentially important days. Often it is the transiting Moon that sets events in motion.

For example, suppose transiting Jupiter is within orb of your natal fifth-house Uranus, an aspect that can mean a windfall. You would then identify a week when two or three inner planets are aspecting the conjunction, even if the contact isn't exact. Next, look to the Moon and identify which days it forms an action aspect (conjunction, square, opposition, semisquare, sesquisquare) to the conjunction. It might be a day when transiting Venus is separating from the conjunction, and Mars is approaching a square to it. Even though the Venus, Mars, and Jupiter contacts are not exact, the transiting Moon will trigger them.

Mercury, Venus, and Mars go through the same retrograde pattern, as do the outer planets. Mercury turns retrograde three or four times each year, Venus about every eighteen months, and Mars about every two years.

Mercury's retrograde cycle can be used to advantage when applying for a job or promotion, for example. A resume submitted when Mercury makes its first contact with a natal or progressed planet can result in an interview on the second contact and a job offer on the third. Retrograde Venus can operate much the same with relationships, but retrograde Mars usually signals frustration and inactivity, a time frame when little, if anything, develops despite other indications.

Use one-degree approaching and separating orbs, and two to three degrees for stations. Mars is the exception, even when direct. It often acts early, up to two degrees before the aspect is exact.

Predictive astrology is thus an "outer" to "inner" process, beginning (after an overview of the natal chart) with progressions and moving on to outer planet transits, eclipses, new and full Moons, and inner transits. It is a step-by-step process that gradually narrows the focus from trend to event, as illustrated in chart 7.

If it sounds complicated, rest assured that it's not. The techniques described here will come to life in succeeding chapters using the natal charts from chapter 3. Read these chapters in sequence. Each builds on the previous to guide you through the predictive process from beginning to end.

3
Natal Chart Delineation

The first step in prediction is natal chart delineation. It gives you insight into the individual's personality, strengths, weaknesses, talents, and more, so you can better predict how the person will respond to progressed and transiting planets (see chapter 2, "Predictive Techniques"). The sample natal chart delineation in this chapter covers general personality traits as well as those related to career. The same chart is used to illustrate predictive techniques in chapters 4, 6, and 8.

Career Path

It takes years for some people to find their way in the world, to discover a career path and pursue it with determination. This is true of David (chart 8), who enrolled in college at age twenty-five after almost a decade of working low-paying jobs, primarily in the food industry. A high school dropout, he earned a GED in his late teens. Today he is a highly respected computer design engineer.

Hemispheres, Quadrants, and Houses

The southern and eastern hemispheres are slightly more prominent in David's chart than the other two, although the planetary emphasis is fairly even throughout his chart:

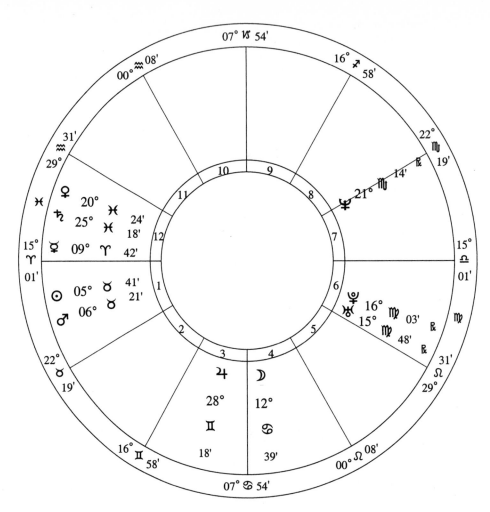

Chart 8
David's Birth Chart
April 26, 1966 / 5:07 AM EDT
Placidus Houses

Southern hemisphere—4 planets

Northern hemisphere—6 planets

Eastern hemisphere—6 planets

Western hemisphere—4 planets

He is self-directed and pursues his wants and needs, with or without others. At times he can be self-centered.

Nine of David's ten planets are in quadrants one, two, and four. This reinforces the emphasis of the northern and eastern hemispheres, so he will have to push himself to network and widen his circle of friendships. Overall, David is independent and self-motivated, and more comfortable in group and family situations than in one-on-one relationships and public life.

The twelfth is the house with the most planets, adding sensitivity, intuition, and compassion. David also can be reclusive, preferring his own company to that of others, and sometimes lacks confidence, especially in social situations.

Elements and Modes

Earth and water are the dominant elements in David's chart:

Fire—1 planet plus the Ascendant

Earth—4 planets plus the Midheaven

Air—1 planet

Water—4 planets

The fire element is weak, but this element gets a boost from the Aries Ascendant and the eastern-hemisphere emphasis, both of which signal initiative and independence. Communication is a weakness with only one planet (Jupiter) in the air element. Jupiter does have more strength, however, because of its placement in the third house of communication; but that also can indicate a rambling talker, a wishful thinker, or one who has difficulty listening to others. On the positive side, Jupiter in the third house indicates a broad, optimistic thinker who perpetually searches for knowledge.

With four planets in water, including the Moon, and three planets in the twelfth house (the natural house of the water sign Pisces), David is intuitive and sensitive. His sixth sense can give him the edge in a wide variety of situations because he's in tune with what others think and feel. Earth is the strongest element. Four planets, including his

Sun, plus the Midheaven, balance the impractical influence of water and add efficiency and common sense. Strong earth also gives him a high need for security.

Mutable signs outnumber cardinal and fixed signs:

Cardinal—2 signs, plus the Ascendant and Midheaven

Fixed—3 signs

Mutable—5 signs

The mutable strength provides an easygoing influence that can be an asset in communication and relationships. This same energy can be detrimental, however, if it manifests as procrastination and indecisiveness, which the water influence also promotes.

The two cardinal planets are reinforced by the Ascendant and Midheaven in the same mode. They signal a self-starter, one interested in launching new endeavors. The three fixed-sign planets add determination and the ability to follow through with what he starts.

The fixed qualities are also strengthened by David's Taurus Sun. The upside of Taurus is staying power, concentration, and a do-or-die approach to goals. Little deters him from his mission once he zeros in on an objective. But the Taurus Sun also shies away from change, preferring stable comfort and security. At times he hesitates to take necessary risks and can be stubbornly set in his ways.

David's Aries Ascendant is at odds with his Taurus Sun. The diverse energy of these two signs can pull him in opposite directions as the cautious, security-minded Taurus battles with the spontaneous, outgoing, risk-taking Aries. It is a dilemma not easily solved and one that likely enters into every major life event and decision. At their best, Aries and Taurus can balance each other, resulting in well-considered calculated risks.

David has the natal setup to achieve this balance because of his Sun-Mars conjunction, undoubtedly the strongest aspect in his chart. This conjunction provides the necessary avenue to blend the Aries/Taurus energy because Mars rules Aries, his rising sign. But the conjunction can as easily be his downfall. Mars in Taurus is, if anything, more stubborn and determined than the Taurus Sun. Directed in a positive way, however, this combination is a powerhouse of energy that can help him achieve the seemingly impossible. This is most evident in personal matters—Sun (self) and Mars (Ascendant ruler)—and in career endeavors—Sun conjunct Mars trine Midheaven, and Sun a co-ruler (with Mercury, ruler of Virgo) of the sixth house of work.

David's sensitive Cancer Moon is supportive of the Sun-Mars conjunction (Moon sextile Sun-Mars), and both Taurus and Cancer favor financial, home, and family security. This combination also promotes an awareness of others that can result in a calm, nurturing quality that people view as a "port in the storm."

The clash between his Moon and rising sign (Moon square the Ascendant/Descendant axis) brings relationship difficulties, most often when he feels threatened by family and security issues. However, the sextile of his Moon to his Sun-Mars conjunction offers the opportunity to involve others in his life in a positive way if he takes the initiative. The choice is his. He can emphasize the lunar-solar contact or succumb to the Moon-Ascendant/Descendant square. The Moon-Mars sextile, although a favorable aspect, can bring out the harshness of the Moon-Ascendant contact because Mars rules the Ascendant. A Moon-Mercury (communication) square adds another layer of difficulty.

Other strong planets in David's chart are the Uranus-Pluto conjunction in opposition to a Venus-Saturn conjunction that squares Jupiter and trines Neptune. These influence his job/career (Saturn rules the Midheaven), as do the Sun-Mars conjunction (the Sun co-rules the sixth house) and the Moon-Mercury square (Mercury co-rules the sixth house and squares the Midheaven).

David's Capricorn Midheaven, ruled by Saturn, which delays action, reflects his late start in zeroing in on a career path. It also suggests the need for a structured, responsible, and secure career that allows him room for growth to fulfill his ambitions. People influenced by Capricorn (and Saturn) also prefer to outline their own plan of action, set their own goals, and work solo. They dislike a boss who hangs over their shoulder. This fits well with the other indicators in David's chart, but again points out the need to develop people skills.

The Venus-Saturn conjunction in the twelfth house repeats the message. Although the ability to work alone is a necessary and desired quality for a computer design engineer, it encourages isolation. And, because Venus rules David's seventh house of relationships and Saturn rules his Midheaven, the conjunction reinforces the importance of other people to his career success. Saturn's involvement also suggests a life lesson that, until learned, will hold him back.

Although David "gave in" to the Jupiter-Saturn square and dropped out of high school, he later met and overcame the challenge of this aspect when he enrolled in college. His Mercury-Midheaven square indicates the same, because Mercury rules early (pre-college) education and its square to the Midheaven represents an obstacle to be overcome to realize his career potential.

David's ambitious Capricorn Midheaven gets an extra push from the Sun-Mars conjunction that trines it. Once he identified his path, nothing stood in his way. The Mercury-Midheaven square, however, also targets communication as a potential career stumbling block. Congenial co-worker relationships and networking contacts are critical to fulfilling his job/career ambitions.

The Sun and Mercury echo the relationship-job theme because they co-rule his sixth house, which is also home to a Uranus-Pluto conjunction that opposes the Venus-Saturn conjunction in the twelfth house (an opposition anywhere in the chart usually reflects a relationship issue). The sixth house conjunction accurately describes his job—Uranus rules computers, and Pluto adds depth and concentration plus the detective talent for writing and de-bugging software code.

But the same conjunction can add volatility in the workplace and subject him to layoffs. Although layoffs are often out of one's control (Pluto), and it is illegal to make such decisions based on personality and friendship, it nevertheless happens. This can be a determining factor for David because Uranus rules his eleventh house of friends and Pluto rules his eighth house of income. Friends/relationships are thus an integral part of job/career and financial success. The conjunction also stresses the importance of networking contacts (eleventh house).

Here again, the Moon and its aspects are the outlet, the solution to resolving the relationship issue. The Uranus-Pluto conjunction sextiles the Moon, which sextiles the Sun-Mars conjunction. However, the Moon also squares the Ascendant and Mercury, and opposes the Midheaven (career). The odds are in David's favor with the Moon in Cancer, its ruling sign and one that is sensitive to others; but a Cancer Moon also easily suffers from hurt feelings. If he can toughen Cancer's shell and take the emotional risk involved in communication and relationships, he will reap the benefits. This also would increase his intuitive abilities.

Solid job relationships and people skills are also key to his earning potential and financial security, as the Venus-Pluto opposition shows in its simplest interpretation. Venus and Pluto rule his second and eighth houses of money.

Note how the same job/career themes are repeated: relationships, communication, finances, ambition. A similar pattern should emerge in any chart overview. Together, the themes reveal the factors that will play a role in life events and predicting their outcome. David's personality and career/job strengths and weaknesses are as follows:

Strengths	**Weaknesses**
Initiative	Relationships
Determination	Headstrong
Ambition	Communication skills
Self-directed	Impulsive
Comfortable working on own	Isolates self at times
Talent for chosen job/career	
Earning potential	
Intuition	

4
Progressions

Progressed planets represent big-picture trends that indicate the general overall influences in your life during a six- to twelve-month period. They offer the first clues to conditions—active or subtle—that can manifest as events.

What you see in the progressed chart is your life unfolding, your potential being fulfilled, including challenges, successes, and periods of change, action, and quiet.

In this chapter we'll build on the interpretation of David's natal chart presented in chapter 3, adding the progressions that indicate current trends.

Career Path

David suddenly decided to return to school in 1991. He came home from work one day and made the announcement. His wife had no inkling of what was on his mind even though she had promoted the idea for a few years.

At the time, David was a termite inspector, the last in a long list of dead-end jobs, as he described them, that ranged from fast food to factory work. (He took the pest control job after being laid off in the spring of 1990.) David had dropped out of high school in the tenth grade and several years later earned a GED.

His original intention was not to earn a bachelor's degree, but to complete an electronics repair course at a community college. After the second quarter, on the advice of a school counselor, he switched to electrical engineering, completed an associate's degree, and transferred to a state university. There, he again switched his field of study, this time to computer engineering.

David's initial career decision was based on his lifelong interest in electronics and science. Computer engineering became his final choice because it offered him "the challenge of combining creativity with logic and design and creating something from nothing," he said. David cites analytical ability, logic, an appreciation for structure, concentration, abstract thinking, creativity, and the ability to work alone as necessary skills and talents for his career.

Decision to Return to School—August 23, 1991

There were many active progressions in David's chart at the time he decided to return to school. This is the kind of lineup an astrologer looks for because it signals a potential major event (chart 9).

- Progressed Sun semisquare natal Ascendant
- Progressed Moon square natal and progressed Uranus-Pluto conjunction
- Progressed Mercury sesquisquare natal Midheaven
- Progressed Pluto conjunct natal Uranus
- Progressed Ascendant sextile natal Saturn

Sign Changes

- Progressed Sun in Gemini (communication, education; ruler of the fifth house of creativity, ego; co-ruler of the sixth house of job/work)

House Changes

- Progressed Moon entering the third house of education

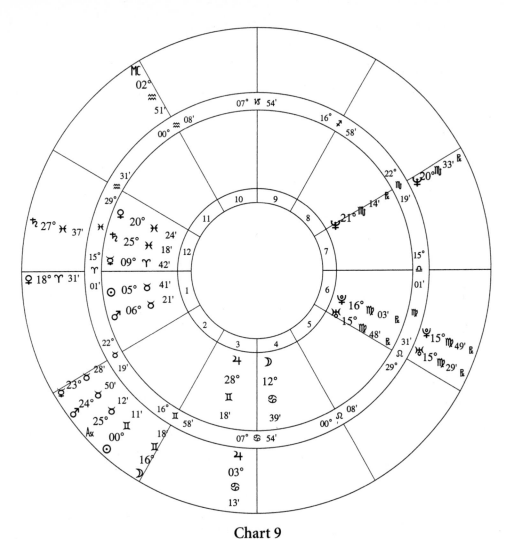

Chart 9
David's Progressed Chart
August 23, 1991 / Placidus Houses

Inner Wheel	**Outer Wheel**
Birth Chart / April 26, 1966	Progressed Chart
5:07 AM EDT	August 23, 1991

Active Planets and Houses

Planet	House Influence
Progressed Sun	Ego; in the second house (self-esteem, money); ruler of the fifth house (creativity, ego); co-ruler of the sixth house (job/work)
Progressed Moon	Emotions; conjunct the third-house (education) cusp; ruler of the fourth house (home, family, beginnings/endings)
Progressed Mercury	Communication; in the second house (self-esteem, money); co-ruler of the sixth house (job/work); ruler of the third house (education)
Natal Saturn	Career, security; in the twelfth house (secret desires); ruler of the tenth house (career, ambition)
Natal Uranus	Change; in the sixth house (job); ruler of the eleventh house (goals); ruler of the twelfth house (secret desires)
Natal Pluto	Transformation, joint resources; ruler of the eighth house (joint resources)
Ascendant	Self
Midheaven	Career, ambition

With progressions and houses spotlighting the self and job/career, a surface glance could lead you to conclude that a job change was likely, possibly a layoff because of the progressed Moon square Uranus-Pluto. But there's more involved here than "a job."

Progressed Mercury sesquisquare the natal Midheaven ties job (sixth house) with education (third house) with career (Midheaven). The third-house education influence (the ninth house rules college and university studies) indicates his initial choice to learn a trade to launch a new job/career. The progressed Sun entering Gemini and the progressed Moon on the cusp of the third house reflect the same.

Progressed Mercury had recently (about a year prior) entered the second house, and the progressed Ascendant had formed a conjunction with progressed Mars about four months before his decision. These influences, combined with the progressed Sun in the second house semisquare the Ascendant and the conjunction of progressed Pluto and natal Uranus, reveal that part of his motivation was to raise his status/self-esteem and earning potential.

Why did he choose the path he did? The progressed Sun (ego) changing signs and in aspect to the natal Aries Ascendant (self) activated the drive necessary to take a risk to better his and his family's life. At the same time, the progressed Ascendant (self) sextile Saturn (Midheaven ruler) stimulated his ambitions.

The conjunction of progressed Pluto and natal Uranus (exact within one minute) is very significant because Pluto moves so slowly. On its own, it signals sudden job developments—when the timing is right. This occurred when the progressed Moon set off this conjunction by square aspect. Notice that it is separating by thirty-one minutes and had been exact about two weeks prior. It also is approaching (one degree, thirty-one minutes) a sesquisquare to the progressed Midheaven.

Why didn't David make the decision to return to school when the progressed lunar square was exact or as it was approaching the square? The same question applies to the progressed lunar sesquisquare, which is not yet within a one-degree orb. The answer is in the timing—the transits—as you will see in chapter 6.

Notice how many progressed aspects lined up at the same time. Although it's impossible to know with any certainty, his life could have taken a different direction had one or two factors been missing. This, of course, is one reason why this example illustrates the value of astrology. It shows a significant turning point, the power of free will and life potential unfolding.

Job Offer—December 12, 1995

David received his bachelor's degree on December 5, 1995, interviewed for a job on December 9, and accepted a position as a design engineer on December 12. Here are the progressed aspects that were active in his chart at the time (chart 10):

- Progressed Mars sextile progressed Saturn
- Progressed Pluto conjunct natal Uranus (exact)
- Progressed Ascendant semisquare natal Ascendant

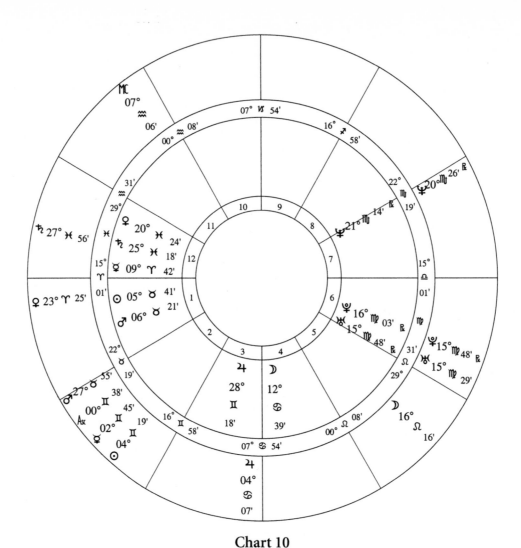

Chart 10
David's Progressed Chart
December 12, 1995 / Placidus Houses

Inner Wheel
Birth Chart / April 26, 1966
5:07 AM EDT

Outer Wheel
Progressed Chart
December 12, 1995

Sign Changes

- Progressed Ascendant in Gemini

Active Planets and Houses

Planet	House Influence
Progressed Mars	Drive, initiative; in the second house (money, self-esteem); ruler of the Ascendant (self); co-ruler of the eighth house (joint resources)
Progressed Saturn	Career, security; in the twelfth house (solitary work); ruler of the tenth house (career, ambition, status)
Natal Uranus	Change; in the sixth house (job); ruler of the eleventh house (goals); ruler of the twelfth house (secret desires)
Progressed Pluto	Transformation, joint resources; in the sixth house (job); ruler of the eighth house (other people's money)
Ascendant	Self

During the time David was in school, progressed Mars (Ascendant ruler) moved from a sextile to natal Saturn (Midheaven ruler) to a sextile with progressed Saturn. He pursued a new career, completed his goal, and redefined his identity. The new job increased his status and income and offered new avenues for learning. He identified the position he wanted and went after it.

The progressed Ascendant, which had sextiled natal Saturn in August 1991, semi-squared the natal Ascendant at the time of graduation and the job offer, signaling initiative and a rise in self-esteem. Of particular interest is that the progressed Ascendant is at 0° Gemini, the same sign and degree of the progressed Sun when David enrolled in college. This is symbolic of his goal and achieving it.

Of equal interest is that progressed Pluto moved the final one minute while he was in school to form an exact conjunction with natal Uranus. The new career would fulfill his job and financial needs.

5

Progressed Planets
in Houses, Signs, and Aspects

Although your natal energy remains the same throughout your lifetime, your birth planets take on the subtle coloration of each succeeding sign and house they enter. By blending the nature of the two, you allow yourself to evolve and experience the wider perspective that each reveals as it enters a new sign or house.

In a normal life span, your progressed Moon moves through the entire zodiac two to three times. Reflect on the life events that occurred approximately twenty-eight years before as it entered the same sign. Although life circumstances and other influences have changed, you can learn much about your emotional responses through hindsight.

Your progressed Sun, Mercury, and Venus travel through two or three signs, and progressed Mars usually through two (three if natal Mars is in a late degree and remains direct). Venus and Mars, however, can stay in the same sign throughout your lifetime, depending on their retrograde cycle. This occurs when Venus or Mars go through the entire retrograde cycle in the same sign.

For example, if you were born with Venus in an early degree of Taurus as the planet was slowing its motion to turn retrograde at 16° Taurus, and later direct at 0° Taurus, it would not enter Gemini until you were more than 120 years old. These unusual situations represent an opportunity to fully understand and incorporate the energy of a planet in a sign in both retrograde and direct motion.

Included in this chapter are the sign/house changes for the progressed inner planets. Refer to chapter 7 for information about the progressed outer planets in signs and houses. The effects of the outer planet transits are similar to progressions, the main difference being the number of years the planet is in each sign/house.

Progressed Sun in the Signs and Houses

Progressed Sun in Aries/First House: Fresh starts and new endeavors appeal to you. But don't jump in headfirst. List the pros and cons, and size up how best to invest your energy for maximum personal or professional gain.

Progressed Sun in Aries/Natal Sun in Aquarius: You're challenged to become more of a risk taker as Aries takes the edge off your fixed nature. Welcome pizzazz and spontaneity, and boldly chase the dreams that were born as your Sun traveled through Pisces. Be assertive yet receptive, and open to change.

Progressed Sun in Aries/Natal Sun in Pisces: Impulsive and action-oriented, Aries energy is foreign to you. View it as a breath of fresh air, the chance to develop the initiative and drive to create your ideal world. Feel your growing confidence, and focus more on your needs, rather than everyone else's.

Progressed Sun in Taurus/Second House: Creature comforts take on added importance. Go one step further. Take a practical look at finances and plan for the long term as security needs rise. Avoid the pack-rat syndrome.

Progressed Sun in Taurus/Natal Sun in Pisces: Your Pisces Sun resonates well with Taurus, which is as practical as it is creative. Profit from both by emphasizing a commonsense, step-by-step approach to life. Combine the confidence you gained from Aries with the endurance of Taurus to build a secure foundation.

Progressed Sun in Taurus/Natal Sun in Aries: The time has come to finish what you started, to add self-discipline to initiative. Learn patience and determination, and refine your impulsive nature to one that's lively yet consistent and dependable. Most of all, move beyond your personal sphere; be sympathetic to others.

Progressed Sun in Gemini/Third House: You feel lighter in spirit and seek social and mental stimulation. Give your curiosity free rein, and study what interests you. Write, read, communicate, and explore.

Progressed Sun in Gemini/Natal Sun in Aries: You experience a sense of freedom, having learned the Taurus lessons of patience and practicality. Now you're set to search for new adventures, but with a more easygoing attitude. Socialize, network, seek outside resources, and expand your information base.

Progressed Sun in Gemini/Natal Sun in Taurus: The energy of the changeable and sometimes frivolous Gemini Sun can be unsettling. Steady and methodical, you're fond of routine, something Gemini shuns. Consider this a chance to break free of self-imposed structures through expanding mental horizons. Meet people.

Progressed Sun in Cancer/Fourth House: Home and family become priorities. Relocate, remodel, and be open to domestic changes. Free your emotions and deal with childhood issues that hold you back.

Progressed Sun in Cancer/Natal Sun in Taurus: You feel more secure on one level, but not on another. Although you have more opportunities to build financial and life stability, doing so requires you to widen your comfort zone. Use your initiative; take action. Home and family offer a built-in safety net for new endeavors and calculated risks. Domestic life centers you.

Progressed Sun in Cancer/Natal Sun in Gemini: Your restless nature is tempered somewhat now that your Sun is in Cancer, and you find value in home, family, and roots. Make your house a haven, a place of retreat where you can get in touch with your feelings. The more emotional baggage you lose, the better. Share your love.

Progressed Sun in Leo/Fifth House: Your focus shifts to personal needs and interests. Use it to discover your creativity. Give birth to a child, idea, or project, something that's an extension of you.

Progressed Sun in Leo/Natal Sun in Gemini: You're ready to tackle the world, thanks to the boost in confidence from Leo. This can be your most creative period, but only if you're committed. Settle down, focus on a few areas of interest, and give them your all. Invite love and children into your life.

Progressed Sun in Leo/Natal Sun in Cancer: Expand your sense of self. Step out of your comfort zone, and stretch yourself and your affections. Gain the self-assurance you need to be your best. Although praise is important, remember that strength and security come from within. Be generous with those you love.

Progressed Sun in Virgo/Sixth House: Raise your health consciousness. Get in shape; tune in and respond to your body's needs. A simpler life attracts you, as does sharing your talents with others.

Progressed Sun in Virgo/Natal Sun in Cancer: Details and the practicalities of daily life consume more of your time. Family or parental health issues also require attention. On a personal level, take a look at your lifestyle. Take action if there's room for improvement, but don't be too hard on yourself.

Progressed Sun in Virgo/Natal Sun in Leo: Your strong Leo Sun limits the effects of Virgo, but it's still influential at times. An emphasis on details and a practical approach are positive; the tendency to be critical of yourself and others is not. Exercise and a healthy diet are important now to relieve work stress.

Progressed Sun in Libra/Seventh House: Extend yourself to people, personally and professionally. Whether single or committed, you're drawn to partnerships and sense that two are better than one.

Progressed Sun in Libra/Natal Sun in Leo: You get more satisfaction from relationships as your affections evolve to a deeper level. Togetherness completes you in a way never before experienced; partnership efforts are rewarding. The Libra influence also helps you step out of the limelight, to spotlight others and give them due credit.

Progressed Sun in Libra/Natal Sun in Virgo: Your reserved nature benefits from Libra's social skills. Observe others, learn the art of small talk, and expand your social circle. Your eye for detail mixes well with Libra's eye for beauty. Use it to bring out your natural flair for design in home decorating and dress.

Progressed Sun in Scorpio/Eighth House: Time alone refreshes and renews you. It's not that other people are less important, but that you first look within for strength. Make self-improvement a goal.

Progressed Sun in Scorpio/Natal Sun in Virgo: Resist the urge to withdraw from the world. Add depth to your relationships instead by merging resources with those closest to you. Financial security also becomes a priority. Use your analytical and research skills to search for the best and safest options.

Progressed Sun in Scorpio/Natal Sun in Libra: Although people and partnerships are a driving force in your life, don't be surprised if you experience a growing need for time alone. It helps you get in touch with your emotions and inner voice, both of which add depth and magnetism to your aura. Get close to people.

Progressed Sun in Sagittarius/Ninth House: You emerge into a wider world as your adventuresome side begins to surface. Seek knowledge for fun or profit and delve into what makes you tick. Learn.

Progressed Sun in Sagittarius/Natal Sun in Libra: A growing sense of optimism encourages you to explore the world. Travel, study, learn, and find inspiration in other cultures and viewpoints. Now is the time to pursue further education if it's been a long-held wish. Do it for personal satisfaction, if for no other reason.

Progressed Sun in Sagittarius/Natal Sun in Scorpio: Sagittarius is dramatically different from your natural guarded and internalized Scorpio energy. Yet this transition serves the purpose of expanding your horizons as you gain insights into and build tolerance for human foibles. Experience all you can, and explore life issues.

Progressed Sun in Capricorn/Tenth House: The urge to excel and raise your worldly status pushes you to achieve. Be seen and heard, and focus on career pinnacles and people who can take you there.

Progressed Sun in Capricorn/Natal Sun in Scorpio: You can step into the power seat and begin to realize long-term goals and achievements. Put Capricorn's initiative and ambition to work for you, but go easy. Emphasize the flexibility you learned from Sagittarius, as well as optimism and open-mindedness. Be responsible.

Progressed Sun in Capricorn/Natal Sun in Sagittarius: Although it stretches you to do so, be smart and rein in your restlessness enough to reap the benefits of Capricorn. Learn to be more practical and systematic and show others they can depend on you. Then your enthusiasm and vision become assets.

Progressed Sun in Aquarius/Eleventh House: Free yourself to experience the new and unusual, and broaden your networking base. Both enhance rather than limit your need for a self-defined lifestyle.

Progressed Sun in Aquarius/Natal Sun in Sagittarius: The free-spirited quality of Aquarius appeals to your independent nature. But Aquarius also challenges you to follow through on commitments. Group endeavors are successful, and friendships become more meaningful. Invite like-minded people into your life.

Progressed Sun in Aquarius/Natal Sun in Capricorn: Let the influence of Aquarius temper your conservative, structured lifestyle. Take a few more risks and be open to new and innovative ideas. Change is refreshing. Socialize more, especially with those who can advance your ambitions. Networking is well worth the effort.

Progressed Sun in Pisces/Twelfth House: Time alone soothes you as it opens up your sensitivities. Get in touch with your feelings, and be receptive to your inner voice. Strive for a healthier lifestyle.

Progressed Sun in Pisces/Natal Sun in Capricorn: Although far different from your natal energy, the Pisces lesson is one of inspiration, compassion, and sensitivity. Be receptive to it. Develop your softer, more emotional side and discover your spirituality and intuition. Doing so can be surprisingly fulfilling.

Progressed Sun in Pisces/Natal Sun in Aquarius: Your altruistic aims fit well with Pisces, a sign that shares your gift of intuition. However, Pisces' emotional and sympathetic traits are more difficult to incorporate into your detached nature. Involve yourself in other people's lives and develop personal sensitivity.

Progressed Moon in the Signs and Houses

Progressed Moon in Aries/First House: You're impulsive! This can be an asset, but not if a quick temper yields rash words. Learn patience and discipline, and temper your opinions. Listen first.

Progressed Moon in Taurus/Second House: You're possessive of people and things, and security issues govern your instincts. Take an occasional risk, even if it's not completely practical. But use your common sense.

Progressed Moon in Gemini/Third House: You're restless amid fluctuating emotions that make it difficult to define your feelings. Go with the flow, experience the entire spectrum, and communicate your feelings.

Progressed Moon in Cancer/Fourth House: Gut feelings and first impressions are on target more often than not. But protect yourself from others and their negative energy. You're more susceptible to it now.

Progressed Moon in Leo/Fifth House: Your responses are more dramatic and also heartfelt. Romance is a high priority, but try to avoid ego-based reactions. Everyone suffers hurt feelings now and then.

Progressed Moon in Virgo/Sixth House: Service projects satisfy your emotional needs and help minimize the tendency to criticize. Work is fulfilling, but keep it in perspective. Break free to socialize.

Progressed Moon in Libra/Seventh House: Peaceful surroundings balance your emotions, as do easygoing people. Reach out to others, and feel the synergy of partnership, love, and mutually supportive endeavors.

Progressed Moon in Scorpio/Eighth House: Feelings run deep, and your emotions are passionate and intense. But don't let them overpower good judgment. Initiate positive personal change.

Progressed Moon in Sagittarius/Ninth House: Adventure, travel, and learning fulfill your emotional needs as you seek action and avoid routine. Insightful dreams open new avenues of personal understanding.

Progressed Moon in Capricorn/Tenth House: Cautious, controlled responses are a plus in business affairs. But don't lose touch with others as you strive for success to fulfill your need for emotional security.

Progressed Moon in Aquarius/Eleventh House: Casual friendships are satisfying, but you have little need to develop them further. Take care, though, that an air of detachment doesn't limit new contacts.

Progressed Moon in Pisces/Twelfth House: Highly intuitive, you're sensitive and receptive to people and your environment. But, be wary. Appearances are often deceiving. Express your creative urges.

Progressed Mercury in the Signs and Houses

Progressed Mercury in Aries/First House: Ideas, opinions—your entire thought process —speed up. But you're also impatient and prone to make snap decisions. Listen first, and speak second. Keep an open mind.

Progressed Mercury in Taurus/Second House: A positive self-image is the first step toward personal and financial security. Do whatever it takes to fill your mind with uplifting thoughts. Common sense guides you.

Progressed Mercury in Gemini/Third House: Curiosity prompts your desire to learn, and you absorb knowledge with ease. But don't spread yourself too thin. Doing so dilutes the benefits. Finish what you start.

Progressed Mercury in Cancer/Fourth House: Emotion colors your thoughts, and you find support in close friends and family. Time at home re-centers you, and issues from the past can be resolved with effort.

Progressed Mercury in Leo/Fifth House: Creativity is your biggest asset now. Nurture it. Seek public-speaking outlets. But keep an open mind and find pleasure in sometimes being the spark rather than the flame.

Progressed Mercury in Virgo/Sixth House: Details, planning, and analysis are your newfound strengths, along with a growing interest in health and service. Profit from them, personally and professionally.

Progressed Mercury in Libra/Seventh House: You're attracted to people, especially to close, one-on-one relationships. Through them you gain an appreciation for a wider range of viewpoints, but try to avoid indecision.

Progressed Mercury in Scorpio/Eighth House: You gain the ability to go beyond the obvious, to sense underlying motives and ferret out the facts. Meditation strengthens your intuition and frees access to your subconscious.

Progressed Mercury in Sagittarius/Ninth House: Daydreams sidetrack you, but they also can provide the impetus to explore new horizons. Use visualization to turn them into concrete goals and go after what you want.

Progressed Mercury in Capricorn/Tenth House: Your powers of concentration increase and you find value in a more practical, logical approach. Use it to advantage in your career, and zero in on long-term objectives.

Progressed Mercury in Aquarius/Eleventh House: You're interested in the new and unusual and seek out intriguing people. Both are avenues to expand your base of social and networking contacts. Use your imagination.

Progressed Mercury in Pisces/Twelfth House: Creative thinking is a plus as long as ideas and solutions are realistic. Heightened intuition adds perception, but take care to protect yourself from negative energy.

Progressed Venus in the Signs and Houses

Progressed Venus in Aries/First House: Impulsive spending sprees are tempting, so adopt a policy to make more than you spend. You're impulsive and passionate in matters of the heart. Be sure before you commit.

Progressed Venus in Taurus/Second House: Steadfast and sensuous in love, you're primed to form a lasting relationship or deepen an existing one. Finances also take a turn for the better if you conserve resources.

Progressed Venus in Gemini/Third House: Flirtatious and popular, socializing moves up a few notches on your list of priorities. Play the field if you're single. Watch your pennies, though. It's easy to squander money.

Progressed Venus in Cancer/Fourth House: Marriage, family, and home life bring pleasure, and parental instincts emerge. You become more financially conservative, and real-estate investments can be profitable.

Progressed Venus in Leo/Fifth House: You attract love and romance, children, and the finer things in life. Find time to play. Social time, exercise, hobbies, and vacations refresh and renew your energy.

Progressed Venus in Virgo/Sixth House: Develop thrifty spending and saving habits, and search for more lucrative job opportunities. However, take care not to criticize coworkers and loved ones. No one and no job is perfect.

Progressed Venus in Libra/Seventh House: An added sense of appreciation for beauty, art, and harmony refines your tastes in surroundings and people. Partnerships are more fulfilling, and social ties expand your world.

Progressed Venus in Scorpio/Eighth House: Significant financial gains can be yours in the years ahead; plan accordingly. Love can be stormy, but also more passionate. Tame jealousy and possessiveness, and open your heart.

Progressed Venus in Sagittarius/Ninth House: Luck is on the upswing in money and love. But an independent, free-wheeling attitude can make it difficult to hang on to either one. Keep that in mind and restrain yourself.

Progressed Venus in Capricorn/Tenth House: You're motivated by money, status, and career advances, all of which can be yours in the coming years. Relationships are influential in achieving your goals.

Progressed Venus in Aquarius/Eleventh House: Mental connections outweigh pure passion in relationships. You also subtly distance yourself from people as independence becomes more important. Be generous yet economical with money.

Progressed Venus in Pisces/Twelfth House: Send out vibes to attract the affection and romance you desire. Try to be practical, though. Love can be deceiving, and finances are easily muddled. Don't take risks with either one.

Progressed Mars in the Signs and Houses

Progressed Mars in Aries/First House: You experience a taste of pure Martian energy in the years to come. Welcome the initiative and drive it adds to your natal Mars, using the combined influence to achieve your goals.

Progressed Mars in Taurus/Second House: Modify your action mode to a slower, steadier pace. In time, it proves effective, and determination sees you through. Incentive is based in the desire for financial security.

Progressed Mars in Gemini/Third House: Restlessness becomes a factor in your life, although not an overpowering one. Find positive outlets in public speaking, classes, reading, and projects. Try not to scatter resources.

Progressed Mars in Cancer/Fourth House: Emotional and security needs affect your actions. This can have a settling influence on your natal energy, but don't let it become a driving force. Express your feelings with kindness.

Progressed Mars in Leo/Fifth House: Your leadership ability begins to emerge and, through it, a growing sense of identity, strength, and willpower. Move into the world, take a few risks, and build your confidence.

Progressed Mars in Virgo/Sixth House: You're more industrious, and find work more satisfying. Pursue a job/career change if you're dissatisfied with your current path. Health-related and mechanical fields can be rewarding.

Progressed Mars in Libra/Seventh House: Cooperative efforts and partnerships help you realize personal and business ambitions. You also invest more of yourself in love relationships and pursue social opportunities.

Progressed Mars in Scorpio/Eighth House: Your aura takes on a subtle intensity that reflects your inner will and resolve to see matters through to conclusion. Don't let stubbornness be your worst enemy, however.

Progressed Mars in Sagittarius/Ninth House: Unleash your spirit of adventure through travel and study. Return to school for a degree, share and gain knowledge, explore your core beliefs, and ask questions.

Progressed Mars in Capricorn/Tenth House: Mars fuels your ambitions, which benefit from a practical yet decisive approach. Commit for the long term. Doing so raises your prospects and betters the outcome.

Progressed Mars in Aquarius/Eleventh House: Groups, friends, and innovative directions are ideal outlets for your budding independence. Each builds on and enhances the others, broadening your natal approach to life.

Progressed Mars in Pisces/Twelfth House: You can become more sympathetic to the plight of other people and can become mired in their emotional issues. Put yourself first; protect your assets and interests. Listen to hunches.

Planetary Aspects

During the course of your lifetime, you'll experience many planetary aspects by progression. Except in rare cases, progressed Mercury and Venus will aspect every natal planet in your chart. The progressed Sun and Moon always do, with the Moon repeating the specific aspect (same sign, house, and aspect) two to three times in a normal life span.

Aspects are classified as action or background, as follows:

Action aspects include the square, opposition, semisquare, and sesquisquare. The conjunction can be easy or difficult, depending upon the planets involved, but it almost always signals action. A Mars-Pluto conjunction, for example, is an action aspect that has negative overtones, suggesting frustration and power plays; a Venus-Mercury conjunction, however, can positively energize your love life.

Background aspects include the sextile and trine, and sometimes the conjunction. These easy aspects can at times initiate action, such as when a trine activates a natal square. In this case, the trine can take the edge off the natal energy or provide an opportunity to resolve it. This is most common when, for example, a natal Venus-Saturn square becomes a progressed Venus-Saturn trine.

The progressed Moon offers ample opportunities to experience its natal energy through sign, house, and aspect. As it moves through the zodiac, it forms a major action aspect (conjunction, square, opposition) to its natal position every seven years. It does the same with sextiles and trines every five years. As this occurs, your natal lunar energy, including aspects, is activated. A progressed Moon in square aspect to a natal Moon-Mercury trine could thus prompt you to take action, while the natal trine would not. And a progressed Moon sextile a natal Moon-Pluto opposition could prompt you to deal with control issues.

A progressed planet in aspect to the same natal one, such as Mercury-Mercury, activates your natal energy and aspects according to the sign and house position of the planets involved. Interplanetary aspects are also influenced according to the natal planetary energy they activate. Interpret them according to the signs and houses where the aspect occurs.

For example, a Sun-Mercury conjunction indicates an active mind that is in large part focused on identity issues. In the fifth house, it could point to the birth of a child; in the seventh house, a marriage; and in the tenth house, a promotion.

In general, progressed planets aspecting themselves have this focus: Sun—ego; Moon —emotions; Mercury—communication, thought process; Venus—relationships, love, money; and Mars—drive, initiative.

Jupiter, Saturn, Uranus, Neptune, and Pluto do not move fast enough by progression to aspect themselves, but their influences, when aspected by other planets, are: Jupiter— expansion, growth; Saturn—restriction, achievement; Uranus—change, mental stimulation; Neptune—spirituality, confusion; and Pluto—change, transformation.

Progressed planets aspect themselves in semisquare, sextile, and square, depending on their rate of movement. The exception is the conjunction, which occurs only if the natal planet is retrograde or turned retrograde after birth. The year it changes direction is significant (see chapter 2), but the conjunction is far more so.

Although the conjunction usually signals an event, its primary importance is on another level. When a planet forms a conjunction after resuming direct motion, it activates the natal potential, releasing the energy to consciousness. Often the individual will realize a long-held desire that he or she was unable to access prior to the conjunction. A planet making a conjunction while retrograde has the opposite effect. It tends to internalize the energy and make it somewhat inaccessible.

Watch for conjunctions involving retrograde planets, which do not occur in every life. Mercury, Venus, and Mars are more likely to form these conjunctions, although Jupiter, Saturn, Uranus, Neptune, and Pluto can do so if they are in a nearly exact aspect at birth.

Progressed planets aspect natal planets and each other. Both are important, but those that involve a natal planet have a greater impact. The progressed-progressed aspects are weaker. The conjunction yields the most concentrated energy, but the square and opposition are equally powerful, with the other aspects being less significant. (The progressed Sun never conjoins natal Sun because it's never retrograde; the progressed Moon conjoins its natal place every twenty-eight years.)

Action Aspects—Square, Opposition, Semisquare, Sesquisquare, Conjunction

Progressed Sun in Action Aspect

Sun-Sun: Your ego comes strongly into play. Use it well, and take care not to alienate others. Enlist their support, and develop relationships. Creative endeavors and hobbies are a good outlet.

Sun-Moon: Emotions pull you in one direction, your self-will in another. Events center around your identity, relationships, and basic life issues. Protect your health and make positive lifestyle changes.

Sun-Venus: You're focused on love, partnerships, and relationships in general. You could marry or strengthen a long-term union, or experience difficulties and separation. Be cautious with money and protect your assets. Stash extra cash that comes your way.

Sun-Mars: Be careful. A fast pace and an invincible attitude are the perfect set-up for an accident. Exercise or other physical activity helps counteract anger, aggression, and sleeplessness. Direct your energy into self-improvement and positive goals.

Sun-Jupiter: You're happy, hopeful, and enthusiastic. Grab opportunities, but don't go out on a limb. Calculated risks are okay; blind optimism is not. Even so, this aspect can signal a silver lining in what otherwise appears to be a tight spot.

Sun-Saturn: There's one sure outcome with this aspect: you get exactly what you deserve. Only you can know what that is. Don't take on everyone else's responsibilities; your own are enough. Counteract fatigue with plenty of rest and sleep.

Sun-Uranus: Ready or not, change is coming. Welcome it, along with an independent streak that signals a shift in your self-perspective. Make it positive. Let enlightenment replace a rising temper, accidents, rebelliousness, and premature action.

Sun-Neptune: Much of what you view as reality at this time is not. Fantasies can lead you astray. Try to penetrate the fog enough to look within in search of new spiritually based personal insights. Full realization comes as this aspect separates.

Sun-Pluto: Power and intensity are the central themes, whether you're on the giving or receiving end. Either way, do something about it. Transform your image rather than someone else's. Be upfront, and avoid manipulation. Give up control to gain success.

Sun-Ascendant: Step out into the world. Be who you want to be and extend yourself to others as people and relationships become more important. Trade favors rather than letting your ego dominate. A love commitment is possible.

Sun-Midheaven: Reach for the top as you focus on career achievements and push yourself to succeed. Recognition comes easily if you live up to your responsibilities. Relocation is likely, possibly because of a promotion.

Progressed Moon in Action Aspect

Moon-Moon: Take note of your emotional responses. They offer clues to your hot buttons and how to better manage them. Explore your feelings, reevaluate family issues, and seek understanding.

Moon-Mercury: Avoid making big decisions and engaging in important negotiations. Emotions can color logic. Express your feelings, but be tactful. You can be drawn into conflict, especially with women.

Moon-Venus: Treat loved ones with kindness, even if you have mixed emotions. Doing so helps promote harmony and understanding. Do the same in your home. Beautify it, but set a budget.

Moon-Mars: Emotions run high, and people and minor matters easily irritate you. Counteract the effect with time alone to relax and re-center. Avoid stressful situations. Think calm and compromise.

Moon-Jupiter: Satisfy your need for freedom through travel and learning, rather than distancing yourself from close relationships. Incorporate the fresh perspective into new goals. Be generous with your time, not your money.

Moon-Saturn: Loneliness and feelings of guilt and regret can take hold under this influence. Try to maintain a realistic view, and avoid the tendency to isolate yourself. Relationships can suffer.

Moon-Uranus: Changing emotions and moods can prompt rash actions you might later regret. Emphasize patience in all you do, and don't jump to conclusions. Fulfill the urge for excitement through a positive, safe outlet.

Moon-Neptune: You're sensitive to people and your environment, both of which can prompt emotional reactions out of the norm. Remember this, and avoid making major commitments. Slights are more perception than reality.

Moon-Pluto: Intense feelings can lead to jealousy and the desire to manipulate emotional situations. Don't go there. Others are likely to do the same to you. Look within yourself. Analyze subconscious motivations.

Moon-Ascendant: Emotions color you and your relationships. Share your feelings without letting them rule your life. Use caution with women. They can be a source of difficulty in your life.

Moon-Midheaven: Family and career matters clash as you attempt to equally divide your time and meet the demands of both. Go for balance. Relocation is possible, or a relative or roommate could move into or out of your house.

Progressed Mercury in Action Aspect

Mercury-Mercury: Center yourself to aid concentration and study, learning and growth. Be somewhat cautious on short trips and errands, and don't share all you know. Communicate selectively.

Mercury-Venus: Play, laugh, socialize, and be happy. Relationships can be a plus if you focus on getting in synch with others. Singles connect with potential love interests; engagement and marriage are possible. Positive thinking attracts abundance.

Mercury-Mars: Strong mental energy generates ideas, but also can lead to snap decisions and angry outbursts. Make it a policy to think before you speak and act, and ease up on the gas pedal during this accident-prone period.

Mercury-Jupiter: Optimism and uplifting thoughts characterize the positive side of this aspect. However, you can get carried away with wishful thinking and quickly find yourself overloaded with activities. Promise only what you can deliver.

Mercury-Saturn: This aspect aids concentration, but it also brings out worries and regrets. Try not to dwell on them. Look forward rather than into the past, except as a learning experience, which is where the real benefit lies. Deal with only your own responsibilities; leave the rest alone.

Mercury-Uranus: Be careful what you toss out in your quest for what's new and different, and make careful moves. Accident potential is high. Direct the energy into school, learning, and innovative ideas, and be alert to flashes of insight that spark fresh viewpoints.

Mercury-Neptune: Confusion rules your thinking, and it's easy to while away hours daydreaming. Find a creative outlet, and explore the world of art and music. Decisions made today are reversed tomorrow; leave yourself an escape hatch.

Mercury-Pluto: You're being forced to change your thinking. That can be positive or negative, depending on how you handle personal power issues and pressure from outside.

Although you're focused to the max, don't let it become tunnel vision. Stay in tune with the big picture.

Mercury-Ascendant: Emphasize a healthy lifestyle, and strive for open, honest communication. Learn the give and take that results in positive relationships as you negotiate for win-win outcomes, personally and professionally.

Mercury-Midheaven: Make an effort to polish and use your public speaking and overall communication skills. Doing so can open avenues to new achievements. In off hours, take a class to build career skills.

Progressed Venus in Action Aspect

Venus-Venus: Use this aspect to advantage. Ask the universe for a zingy love life with someone new or your mate. Pour on the TLC. Accept or offer a marriage proposal, but marry only if you're sure and your heart is relatively objective. Watch the sweets and your waistline; try not to indulge.

Venus-Mars: Find your way into someone's heart or let someone into yours, rather than letting underlying relationship tensions erupt. But be discriminating if you're single. Passion is one thing, but satisfying an itch is quite another, especially one based solely on physical attraction.

Venus-Jupiter: Whether it's money or love, rein yourself in a little. Pleasure works to a point; after that, it's too much of a good thing. Set limits, and add a dose of reality. Then, partnerships, love, engagements, and weddings get a thumbs-up.

Venus-Saturn: If you're already in a relationship, this aspect can either strengthen it or add a distinct chill. It's not the best for start-ups or reuniting with old loves, but it can help you reassess and realign finances. Do what's necessary to pay off debt.

Venus-Uranus: New relationships sparkle with love at first sight, which falls right in line with your need for excitement and change. Don't leap out of or into a partnership, though, until the aspect passes. Find other ways to satisfy your need for independence. A windfall is possible.

Venus-Neptune: You're lost in an idealistic fantasy, one that defines romance at its best. The question is whether it's true or false, but you won't know until the aspect passes. Self-deception is the culprit in love and money as you ignore reality. Channel the energy into creativity.

Venus-Pluto: Even if you're not naturally inclined, this aspect encourages jealousy and possessiveness, not just of people, but also of things. You can easily become obsessed with either. Get in touch with what you value personally, in life and in others.

Venus-Ascendant: Love, romance, and marriage can sweep you off your feet. Or you could decide to move on, depending on your outlook and what you really want out of life. Attract all the good you deserve.

Venus-Midheaven: A significant boost in popularity can land you a top job or a promotion. Meet expectations to ensure that it lasts. A new or redecorated home can also be yours, possibly with a new mate.

Progressed Mars in Action Aspect

Mars-Mars: Slow down! Program rest time into your busy life, even if it means letting things go. You can easily overdo it now, make mistakes, and invite accidents. Think before you act and speak. Be good to yourself.

Mars-Jupiter: Your high energy is great for new ventures and high productivity, and calculated risks can turn out amazingly well. Think things through first, however; excessive optimism can get the best of you.

Mars-Saturn: Frustration and delays require persistence, patience, and hard work. Keep at it and eventually you'll move through roadblocks to success. Don't try to take the easy way out, though. Live up to your responsibilities.

Mars-Uranus: Overprogramming leads to stress, nervous tension prompts haste and carelessness. The combination can spark accidents and a short temper. Use exercise as an antidote, and focus on positive personal change and self-expression.

Mars-Neptune: Confusion dominates. You're unsure which path to pursue, which direction to take, literally and figuratively. Find a creative outlet to divert the energy. Major endeavors are sidetracked, and even the best efforts dissipate into the mist.

Mars-Pluto: Positive passions can lead to achievement. Obsession and power plays undermine your position. The more you rebel against the boss or other authority figures, the worse the outcome. Claim your own power without the dramatics.

Mars-Ascendant: Temper your high energy with a little caution. The fast pace increases accident potential. Do what's necessary to ensure that sleep doesn't elude you. It's more important now than ever.

Mars-Midheaven: You could find yourself in fierce competition with others, as well as in the middle of controversy. Think before you speak and act, especially with the boss and other authority figures. Emphasize courtesy and tact.

Progressed Jupiter in Action Aspect

Jupiter-Jupiter: Be alert to opportunities, but try not to jump in feet first. Get the facts first. Luck can be on your side, or not. Don't count on it; welcome it when it arrives. Remember that you can make your own luck. Be happy, think positive, learn, grow, travel, and broaden your horizons.

Jupiter-Saturn: It's easy to become overloaded with responsibilities. Set priorities, and say no to optional items. Then you can pursue promising opportunities, all of which require effort to earn rewards. Take reasonable risks in career and business; broaden your knowledge.

Jupiter-Uranus: Known for delivering windfalls and lucky breaks, this aspect can put you in the right place at the right time. But be selective, and choose the best of the best, whatever will bring you maximum gain for reasonable effort. Have faith in your decisions.

Jupiter-Neptune: Romance and promises can be the real thing. They also can be pipe dreams leading you on a merry chase in search of rainbows. Enjoy the fun and laughter in fantasyland, knowing it's probably smoke and mirrors. Discover your creative self.

Jupiter-Pluto: You can move mountains with this aspect, which can deliver unparalleled success. Decide what you want beforehand and how you'll get it. Then use luck and willpower rather than manipulation and control.

Jupiter-Ascendant: Now is not the time to overindulge in anything. It is, however, an ideal period for personal growth and learning. Learn all you can about yourself, other people, and the world around you.

Jupiter-Midheaven: The urge to excel is strong, but so is the temptation to take on more than you can realistically handle. This applies to career endeavors as well as home ownership. Be smart. Buy less than you can afford.

Progressed Saturn in Action Aspect

Saturn-Saturn: Heavy responsibilities and minimal progress can get you down. Guard against this by developing patience and understanding. Measure past success, and set future goals. Career success is possible at this time.

Saturn-Uranus: It's time for a change. The old ways no longer work even though there's security in the status quo. Let go of the past and create a new reality when sudden change is thrust upon you. Through it, you develop newfound independence.

Saturn-Neptune: With one foot in reality and the other in a dream world, it's difficult to know where to walk. You learn that life is a matter of perception. Don't avoid reality, even if it means making tough decisions related to those you love. Avoid making career decisions.

Saturn-Pluto: The more you try to control events, the more frustration you experience. Like other difficult Saturn aspects, this one signifies major change, often career-related. With Pluto involved, events are essentially out of your control. Pick up the pieces and move on.

Saturn-Ascendant: Be especially good to yourself. Get a health check-up and plenty of sleep, and don't push yourself. Give close relationships the attention they need and don't be too quick to run from difficulties.

Saturn-Midheaven: Work hard, live up to your responsibilities, and follow the career rules. Doing so increases your odds of success. Family matters take more of your time, and you should be cautious in property deals.

Progressed Uranus in Action Aspect

Uranus-Uranus: The only constant is change. Be prepared for anything and everything, as well as a quest for independence. Resist the urge, however, to toss out all of the old in favor of the new. Aim for self-improvement.

Uranus-Neptune: Excellent for creativity, intuition, and innovation, this aspect (and others involving Neptune) is often found where drugs and alcohol are involved. Irresponsibility is also a factor when its negative side dominates.

Uranus-Pluto: A desire for personal freedom and independence can push you to break free of all restraints, but such changes are irrevocable. This aspect also can turn your world upside down when you're caught in the middle of power shifts. Regroup and restart.

Uranus-Ascendant: Personal and relationship changes are on the horizon. Try to blend them rather than let your interests supersede those of a union. However, if all avenues lead to closed doors, do what is ultimately best for you.

Uranus-Midheaven: Career changes are a given, so try to set yourself up for the best possible outcome. Networking is especially valuable. Relocation or major household change is also likely to fulfill your desire for what's new and different.

Progressed Neptune in Action Aspect

Neptune-Neptune: Get creative, and explore your hidden talents. It's a positive outlet for this aspect, which can leave you feeling at loose ends with no answers and nowhere to go. Seek a spiritual perspective.

Neptune-Pluto: As with other aspects involving Pluto, there's little you can do to control the events around you. With Neptune, the familiar dissipates, and disillusionment can set in. Seek creative solutions as you move through the maze.

Neptune-Ascendant: Redefine yourself and your approach to relationships. Look at what works and what doesn't, and how you can better fulfill both needs. Be prepared to see some people in an entirely different light.

Neptune-Midheaven: The professional goal you seek to achieve can slip through your fingers or materialize out of thin air. A word of caution: be sure it's real. Make your mark in creative endeavors. Family issues require attention.

Progressed Pluto in Action Aspect

Pluto-Pluto: Resist the urge to toss everything out and start over, except in a symbolic way. Self-improvement and positive change should be your goals, along with a more complete understanding of what makes you tick.

Pluto-Ascendant: Power issues require resolution. Take charge of your life, empower yourself, and refuse to let others direct your moves. How you handle both determines the level of personal transformation you achieve.

Pluto-Midheaven: You can rise to the top or be one of many whose lives are disrupted by matters out of their control. Focus on using this time to review and revise career ambitions. Be brave enough to move in a totally new direction.

Background Aspects—Sextile, Trine, Conjunction

Progressed Sun in Background Aspect

Sun-Sun: You and your life are in synch. Assert yourself, and find new directions for your talents and an outlet for your developing leadership.

Sun-Moon: You feel and look good, on an even keel with emotions and identity in balance. Conditions are positive for action in other areas.

Sun-Mercury: Your thinking is on track, and you make good decisions based on personal needs. Communication is an asset.

Sun-Venus: Pleasure and comfort are satisfying, as is socializing, but try to limit self-indulgence. It's best to give as much as you get.

Sun-Mars: You're in a high-energy phase, on the move and pouring your energy into what you want. This makes it easier to deal with life events.

Sun-Jupiter: Popularity rises along with optimism and positive thinking. Keep it in perspective, and push for growth. Limit excesses.

Sun-Saturn: Steady, slow progress yields results with patience. Life may not be exciting, but you feel grounded. Limit responsibilities to your own.

Sun-Uranus: You're open to change, so go beyond the same old thing. Focus on possibilities that can produce positive personal changes.

Sun-Neptune: Creativity and intuition are high, and visualization can produce amazing results. Use meditation to access your inner voice.

Sun-Pluto: You have the will and determination to go after what you want. Important people provide contacts that lead to success. Return the favor.

Sun-Ascendant: People see and sense your rising confidence, and relationships are easygoing. Tap into your natural leadership ability.

Sun-Midheaven: Career and family bring happiness, and life perks along. Take advantage of opportunities to mix and mingle with important people.

Progressed Moon in Background Aspect

Moon-Moon: Exchange favors, socialize, and enjoy the positive energy flow between you and others that comes from being in tune with yourself.

Moon-Mercury: Communicate your feelings during this upbeat period that puts you and others on the same wavelength.

Moon-Venus: Relationships move along at an easy pace, but this aspect also inclines toward laziness and self-indulgence. Finances are positive.

Moon-Mars: You easily push your own agenda, and nicely so. People are happy to help. Act on your emotions and passions.

Moon-Jupiter: The ultimate feel-good aspect surrounds you with optimism, luck, and hope. Add your efforts to ensure that things go your way.

Moon-Saturn: You're in control of your feelings and approach life and career with a realistic view. Recognize and deal with emotional baggage.

Moon-Uranus: Invite some new faces and friendships into your life. Some of them could be lucky networking contacts. Group endeavors open doors.

Moon-Neptune: Romantic and intuitive, you're in synch with your heart and inner voice. Succumb to fantasy via movies, music, and poetry.

Moon-Pluto: You feel strong and powerful, but steer clear of manipulative moves and situations, whether you're the giver or receiver. Own your feelings.

Moon-Ascendant: Seek women who can grant favors, and enjoy this upbeat period during which you're in tune with your emotions and inner self.

Moon-Midheaven: The recognition you seek comes easily, and home life is especially satisfying. Reconnect with relatives.

Progressed Mercury in Background Aspect

Mercury-Mercury: Mental energy and communication are your greatest assets at this time. Use both to advantage to get what you want.

Mercury-Venus: Tact, grace, and charm are yours. Relationships benefit from communication, and you get most everything you ask for, including money.

Mercury-Mars: Quick thinking aids studies, public speaking, and new endeavors. Ideas are great, but only if you act on them.

Mercury-Jupiter: You can turn minuses into pluses with Jupiter luck, and deliver what you promise. Find a way to capitalize on great ideas.

Mercury-Saturn: Logical thinking and concentration are a plus, especially in business situations and interviews. Past deeds pay off.

Mercury-Uranus: Innovative thinking and intuition lead you in the right direction. Tale a class, join a group, and meet people.

Mercury-Neptune: Intuition is on target. Trust it in what you say and think, and trust your gut feelings about people. Night and day dreams offer insight.

Mercury-Pluto: Your powers of persuasion are at their best. This comes in handy in presentations and meetings. Research yields all the facts.

Mercury-Ascendant: The right words and the best ideas come to you effortlessly. Together, they give you the edge in almost every situation.

Mercury-Midheaven: Take a class and learn all you can, rather than relying solely on your quick wit. It pays off in the long run.

Progressed Venus in Background Aspect

Venus-Venus: You can attract love and money with little effort, so resist this potential lazy streak and pursue your heart's desire.

Venus-Mars: Love and other relationships benefit from this aspect, which can invite new people into your life. Seek them out. Set spending limits.

Venus-Jupiter: Fun and socializing are first on your agenda. Go beyond that. Let this lucky combination add success in other areas. Watch your budget.

Venus-Saturn: Solid relationships become more so, but others prompt second thoughts. A little distance adds perspective. Save money.

Venus-Uranus: Commitment is the last thing on your mind with so many love interests to choose from. Enjoy the sparks of attraction, and buy a lottery ticket.

Venus-Neptune: You crave romance in any form. Find it with your mate, someone new, or a steamy novel. Money slips through your fingers.

Venus-Pluto: You have the power to attract love and money. Loans are usually approved, and investments can increase your net worth.

Venus-Ascendant: Love is lovely, life is pleasant, and you can attract almost anything your heart desires. People are generous; return the favor.

Venus-Midheaven: Home life is all you could wish for, and favorable career reviews can open the avenue to future gains.

Mars in Background Aspect

Mars-Mars: Act quickly and decisively, but also wisely during this time of high initiative. Set clear goals and capitalize on your talents.

Mars-Jupiter: Energy and good luck are on your side, and this aspect lends both to current endeavors. Take a few risks.

Mars-Saturn: Although the pace is slower than you wish, steady effort leads to success. Move around obstacles until you meet your objective.

Mars-Uranus: Opportunities abound, and you can zero in on those with the most potential. Add your own unique twist to make the most of it.

Mars-Neptune: Hunches pay off if you listen and act on them. The more you trust yourself, the better the outcome. Help others.

Mars-Pluto: Besides providing help to find a way around roadblocks, this aspect gives you the power to make things happen.

Mars-Ascendant: Added energy helps you maintain a steady pace and increases the chances for passion and love.

Mars-Midheaven: Think about where you're headed career-wise because now is the time to lay a foundation for the future.

Progressed Jupiter in Background Aspect

Jupiter-Jupiter: Luck is with you if you make the most of this time. Grab opportunities for growth and success, rather than going along for the ride.

Jupiter-Saturn: Optimism and reality balance one other, giving you a rational yet hopeful view of any situation. Profit from business and study.

Jupiter-Uranus: This aspect adds luck to most any event. It could be a big bonus, a golden opportunity, or someone who smoothes your path.

Jupiter-Neptune: Faith and optimism, self-help groups, worthy causes, and spiritual insights open you up to new truths and ease life challenges.

Jupiter-Pluto: Invest your energy and your wishes carefully. This fortunate aspect can deliver it all and more if you put your mind to it.

Jupiter-Ascendant: Direct this lucky influence to advantage, rather than drifting along on a wave of optimism and good fortune.

Jupiter-Midheaven: A new home and career gains can fall in your lap as a long-term lucky period begins to unfold.

Progressed Saturn in Background Aspect

Saturn-Saturn: Responsibility and reward go hand in hand, and especially favor career success and real estate. Take a step up in the world.

Saturn-Uranus: Saturn sets the boundaries and Uranus offers the way to adapt changes to suit you. Add innovation and imagination.

Saturn-Neptune: Structure takes on a softer aura that lets you bend the rules and allow room for creativity and inspiration. Be benevolent.

Saturn-Pluto: This aspect helps you set plans in motion for the long term. Plan your rise to the top, and get acquainted with decision makers.

Saturn-Ascendant: Your course is steady, although without glamour. You're content with that and the solid relationships that surround you.

Saturn-Midheaven: Take on extra career responsibilities as an investment in your future. Real estate can be an excellent investment now.

Progressed Uranus in Background Aspect

Uranus-Uranus: Network, socialize, and get involved in a like-minded group. Each can be an avenue to unexpected gain and new insights.

Uranus-Neptune: Get in touch with your personal muse. Write poetry, study metaphysics, volunteer, and find your creativity.

Uranus-Pluto: Internal and external events spark positive personal changes. Friends and groups are influential.

Uranus-Ascendant: Independence works exceptionally well for you now, and it's also a plus in relationships. Be yourself.

Uranus-Midheaven: Career/job changes you make now are positive. The same is true of your home life. Relocate or redo your space.

Progressed Neptune in Background Aspect

Neptune-Neptune: Imagination and creativity are a plus, and your thoughts and opinions subtly shift to new personal truths. Welcome them.

Neptune-Pluto: Your spiritual base, as well as many of your beliefs, evolve as outside influences alter your worldview.

Neptune-Ascendant: Intuition and creativity are yours for the asking. Listen to the first and use the second, and develop both.

Neptune-Midheaven: Re-create your career and home environments to reflect your definition of the ideal. Be creative.

Progressed Pluto in Background Aspect

Pluto-Pluto: You have the power to make things happen. Use it to positively reshape your personal world for the better.

Pluto-Ascendant: Use Pluto's power to adapt and change yourself and your relationships for the better. It comes easily now.

Pluto-Midheaven: Pulling strings is easy because you have the strength. Do so wisely, however. Empower others to achieve success.

6

Outer Planet Transits
and Eclipses

The outer planet transits and solar and lunar eclipses narrow the predictive focus even further and provide the initial clues to event timing.

Progressions set the trends for about a year, and eclipses spotlight a period of six to twelve months. The outer planet transits indicate a time frame of a few weeks to a few months. They also signal beginning, intermediate, and final steps as they station (turn retrograde or direct) and transit back and forth over natal and progressed planets.

The outer transiting planets are almost always within a one-degree orb when the inner transiting planets set off the outer planet energy. Pluto is the exception; its influence is sometimes felt from an approaching orb of three to four degrees. It's not uncommon for an outer planet transit to be exact at the time of an event, but it's also not the norm. So don't expect to see the effects of outer planet transits on the day they're exact.

What you will see every time are the outer planet transits setting off natal planetary energy or progressed planets in aspect to progressed and natal planets. This happens as a transiting planet contacts a planet involved in a single natal or progressed planetary aspect, such as a square, or a planet that's part of a configuration, such as a t-square. Ultimately, though, it is the natal energy that is being activated.

No two charts are the same, and neither is the combination of outer planet transits and progressed and natal planets. During some events, the outer planet transits set off nearly every progressed aspect. In others, the transits and their direct/retrograde/stationary patterns alone reveal the clearest message. In each case, the secret is to look for the transit connection that repeats the trends seen in the progressed aspects.

Now let's look at how the eclipses and outer planet transits activated David's chart.

Career Path

David's job/career planets and angles are the Sun (sixth-house co-ruler), Uranus-Pluto (in the sixth house), Mercury (sixth-house co-ruler), Saturn (Midheaven ruler), Uranus (progressed Midheaven ruler), and the Midheaven. Each of these, whether progressed, natal, or both, was aspected in both 1991 and 1995.

Decision to Return to School—August 23, 1991

David's sudden decision to return to school only appeared to be sudden. He had actually been thinking about it for some time, but, as is true of most life events, action happens when the time is right and the planets create the appropriate conditions.

One eclipse occurred in June 1991, and two others the next month. All three pushed David's decision to the forefront. The June 27, 1991, lunar eclipse at 5°00' Capricorn was conjunct his natal Midheaven from the ninth house of higher education, square natal Mercury, and trine his first-house natal Sun and Mars. Two weeks later, the July 11 solar eclipse at 18°59' Cancer squared his natal Ascendant and sextiled natal/progressed Uranus and Pluto in the sixth house of work. The third eclipse at 3°16' Aquarius on July 26 was conjunct his progressed Midheaven and square natal Sun and Mars. This trio of eclipses activated his career (Midheaven), job planets (Uranus, Pluto, Sun, Mercury), and personal incentive and initiative (Ascendant, Sun, Mars).

A long list of outer planet aspects were active at the time of David's decision and the period leading up to it (chart 11). It is rare to see aspects from every outer planet at the time of an event, and this fact alone indicates a major life development.

- Transiting Jupiter square progressed Mercury (separating)
- Transiting Jupiter square progressed Mars (separating)

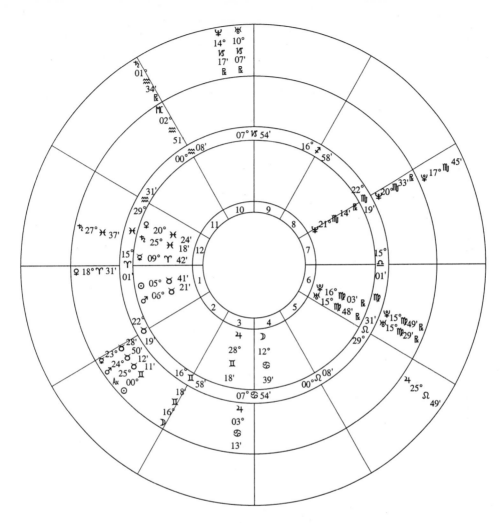

Chart 11
David's Progressed Chart with Transits
August 23, 1991 / Placidus Houses

Inner Wheel	Middle Wheel	Outer Wheel
Birth Chart	Progressed Chart	Transits
April 26, 1966	August 23, 1991	August 23, 1991
5:07 AM EDT		

- Transiting Jupiter square progressed Ascendant
- Transiting Saturn trine progressed Sun
- Transiting Saturn sesquisquare progressed Moon
- Transiting Saturn sesquisquare natal/progressed Uranus-Pluto
- Transiting Saturn conjunct progressed Midheaven (approaching)
- Transiting Uranus conjunct natal Midheaven (separating)
- Transiting Uranus sesquisquare progressed Mercury (separating)
- Transiting Uranus sesquisquare progressed Mars
- Transiting Uranus square progressed Ascendant
- Transiting Neptune trine natal/progressed Uranus-Pluto (approaching)
- Transiting Neptune square natal Ascendant/Descendant
- Transiting Pluto conjunct natal/progressed Neptune

Transiting Jupiter, ruler of David's ninth house, had squared his progressed Mercury and Mars earlier in August. However, it wasn't until Jupiter squared the progressed Ascendant that he took action—with an extra push from transiting Uranus, which was sesquisquare the progressed Ascendant and progressed Mars (Ascendant ruler).

The transit of Uranus over his Midheaven, which began in February 1990 and concluded in November 1990, had a preliminary role in his decision-making process. He was laid off during that time and moved on to a new job.

The idea to return to school gradually took hold as transiting Uranus first squared his natal Mercury (ruler of the third house of education) in April 1990 when it stationed to turn retrograde at 9°35' Capricorn. It made another station, this one direct, in September 1991, at 9°50' Capricorn, also square natal Mercury. During the same time frame, Uranus was sesquisquare progressed Mercury.

Transiting Saturn, David's career planet, reflects the length of time it took for the school idea to germinate and come to fruition. Saturn was conjunct progressed Midheaven in March and July 1991. It would station in October 1991 at 0°12' Aquarius, exactly trine progressed Sun, ruler of David's sixth house of work. Saturn was also sesquisquare natal/progressed Uranus-Pluto in the sixth house when he made the decision to help change his perspective from "job" to "job/career."

This example also points out the value of the progressed Moon as a timer. Saturn was sesquisquare the progressed Moon and natal/progressed Uranus-Pluto, setting off the progressed Moon's square to Uranus-Pluto. Saturn did the same with the progressed Sun-Ascendant semisquare, and Neptune squared natal Ascendant.

Job Offer—December 12, 1995

Although job interviews and offers are specific events, they too are influenced by the trends. If the eclipses and progressed and transiting outer planets are unfavorable, job developments won't materialize or at least not as hoped for. Keep this in mind as you look at the outer planet transits. This example focuses on the transiting planets on the day of the job offer (chart 12).

The October 8, 1995, lunar eclipse at 14°54' Aries was conjunct David's Ascendant. On October 24, 1995, a solar eclipse at 0°18' Scorpio opposed David's natal Sun-Mars conjunction and semisquared natal/progressed Uranus-Pluto.

As was true in 1991, every transiting outer planet aspected David's chart (chart 12):

- Transiting Jupiter square natal Saturn
- Transiting Saturn semisquare natal Sun-Mars (approaching; Saturn stationed direct on November 12, 1995, at 18°00' Pisces)
- Transiting Saturn opposition natal/progressed Uranus-Pluto (separating)
- Transiting Saturn semisquare progressed Midheaven (separating)
- Transiting Uranus trine progressed Mars
- Transiting Uranus sextile progressed Saturn
- Transiting Uranus sesquisquare natal/progressed Uranus-Pluto (approaching)
- Transiting Neptune sextile natal Saturn (approaching)
- Transiting Pluto opposition progressed Mercury (approaching)
- Transiting Pluto conjunct/opposition progressed Descendant/Ascendant

The progressed Mars–progressed Saturn sextile benefited from transiting Uranus in sextile/trine to it, creating more positive energy for this job/career trend. Uranus also was approaching a sesquisquare to natal/progressed Uranus-Pluto, which would be exact when he started the job at the end of January 1996.

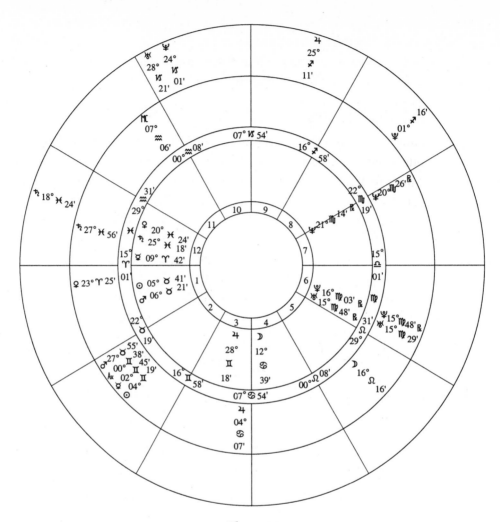

Chart 12
David's Progressed Chart with Transits
December 12, 1995 / Placidus Houses

Inner Wheel	Middle Wheel	Outer Wheel
Birth Chart	Progressed Chart	Transits
April 26, 1966	December 12, 1995	December 12, 1995
5:07 AM EDT		

Transiting Jupiter added its influence with a square to natal Saturn, an aspect that brings good luck in career endeavors if one has earned it.

The transiting Saturn-Neptune sextile reflects David's high hopes and ideals for the new job/career. That they were unrealistic proved to be true. The new position wasn't exactly as he had envisioned it, but it did offer the opportunity to develop co-worker relationships because the transits activated his natal Venus-Saturn-Neptune trine, which in turn brought the natal Venus-Jupiter-Saturn square into focus.

The two Pluto aspects, long-term trends that would continue through the summer of 1997, reflect increased income (second/eighth houses) as well as relationships. Pluto in action aspect to the progressed Ascendant/Descendant adds a negative interpretation to the aforementioned transiting Saturn-Neptune influence. Relationship challenges with co-workers could be expected and did occur in that he had difficulty forming close friendships on the job.

7

Outer Planet Transits, Houses, and Aspects

Like progressions, the outer planet transits signal trends, usually centered around one or two areas of life, such as career, relationships, family, and personal growth. Keep this in mind as you read about the transits to your chart. Consider each transit individually and as a part of a larger picture, and blend them to identify solutions and opportunities.

Jupiter Transits

Jupiter, the planet of expansion and good fortune, always lives up to its reputation in one way or another. This might or might not be to your benefit. Jupiter can personify luck and bring a lottery win, a major promotion, love, money, travel, and more. But sometimes it delivers too much of a good thing. It also can promise the world, only to have the last laugh.

At its best, Jupiter signals windows of opportunity, times when you can make your own luck. This is true even when, for example, a Jupiter-Uranus aspect delivers a lucky break out of the blue. It's still up to you and your free will to act on it, to follow up on a job opening, shop a sale, invite a romantic interest to dinner, or purchase a winning lottery ticket.

Jupiter is also noted for excess, a trait that can cause ironic twists, such as when a Jupiter-Neptune aspect brings you new carpeting after a household flood. It also can dangle carrot-like promises, unrealistically raising your hopes.

In general, though, Jupiter does take the edge off difficult aspects and adds luck to beneficial ones. Just don't count on it to bail you out of every situation.

Jupiter transits the zodiac once every twelve years, spending approximately one year in each sign and house of the horoscope.

Jupiter in the Houses

Jupiter in the First House: An overall lucky year, you find new avenues of personal expression, experiences, and growth. Creativity and confidence fill you with optimism and a willingness to move outside your comfort zone.

Jupiter in the Second House: Income rises, but so do expenses. Resist spending sprees, and use resources wisely. Also target this year as one for self-improvement. The bottom line: you are your greatest asset.

Jupiter in the Third House: The need for mental stimulation pushes you toward short-term classes, short trips, and reading. Think positive; stretch your mind. You also can strengthen ties with siblings and other relatives.

Jupiter in the Fourth House: A growing interest in the domestic scene motivates you to purchase property, relocate, or redecorate, possibly because of an addition to the family. Learn do-it-yourself skills. Entertain.

Jupiter in the Fifth House: Creativity is high, and you're in a social, fun-loving period that favors romance. Date, meet new people, and delight in time spent with children. Investments and hobby-based cottage industries can be profitable.

Jupiter in the Sixth House: Work and volunteer efforts are satisfying, but you also can take on too much. A healthier lifestyle is a better choice. A job search can be successful. Seek a position that promises growth.

Jupiter in the Seventh House: Love relationships and other partnerships are fulfilling, and lucky contacts invite more of the same. Learn from others and trade favors. Marriage is possible, but not a given.

Jupiter in the Eighth House: This year-long financial trend is positive as you benefit from other people's resources—a pay raise, an inheritance, a loan, insurance, and investments. Live within your means and increase your overall net worth.

Jupiter in the Ninth House: Teach, learn, travel, and explore to broaden your perspective. Metaphysical studies are enlightening as they lead to a greater depth of self-understanding. Handle routine legal matters.

Jupiter in the Tenth House: Confidence in your career skills and talents can result in a promotion, increased status, and awards. This year also can bring lucky breaks and a career shift to a related field.

Jupiter in the Eleventh House: Widen your circle of personal and professional contacts through group activities and friends. Many of them help redefine and shape your evolving goals.

Jupiter in the Twelfth House: Your guardian angel comes in many forms, from unseen helpers to luck when you most need it. Access and develop your intuition through meditation. Release subconscious thoughts.

Jupiter Action Aspects—Conjunction, Opposition, Square, Semisquare, Sesquisquare

Jupiter-Sun: Opportunity and good fortune prevail, but don't push your luck. Any form of excess, including financial extravagance and foolish schemes, is risky. Well thought-out new endeavors do well.

Jupiter-Moon: You're upbeat, optimistic, and generous. Stop there and don't let yourself slip into self-indulgence. Satisfy your emotional needs through people contact, rather than spending or eating.

Jupiter-Mercury: Positive thinking and a thirst for knowledge can generate big ideas. Be sure they're practical. It's easy to overestimate your ability to deliver. Listen more than you talk.

Jupiter-Venus: Relationships bring you pleasure, and you welcome a new romance, engagement, or marriage. Stay away from sweets, spending sprees, and investments, however.

Jupiter-Mars: Your high energy and ambitions are an asset as long as you don't overdo. Think before you act, because overconfidence can cancel the gain. Be efficient, and take only calculated risks.

Jupiter-Jupiter: This influence is more fortunate than not, but you're nevertheless prone to over-optimism, which can be a plus or minus. Use common sense, and strive for balance. Finances are either up or down, depending upon your decisions. Have a safety net.

Jupiter-Saturn: This combination challenges you to balance expansion and contraction, growth and caution. Resist the urge to leap in either direction. Further education can lead to career advancement.

Jupiter-Uranus: Cross your fingers! Sudden opportunities and windfalls can be yours. Your need for excitement, however, can prompt careless actions that undermine the good. Network through groups and friends.

Jupiter-Neptune: You're on a spiritual, idealistic plane that can put you at a disadvantage in mundane affairs. Beware of deception and false promises, and be cautious with money. Volunteer for a good cause.

Jupiter-Pluto: Ambition drives you. That's advantageous as long as you keep your strength in perspective. Don't push your agenda too strongly. You also can be caught in the middle of a power struggle.

Jupiter-Ascendant: Invite new people into your life, and be generous with your time and talents. Others return your generosity twice over. Travel and growth are positive, as are close relationships and marriage.

Jupiter-Midheaven: Career gains are likely if they're based on realistic goals. Analyze before you act. Do the same with your home. Purchase property, redecorate, or add furnishings—but only what you can afford.

Jupiter Background Aspects—Sextile, Trine, Conjunction

Jupiter-Sun: You're surrounded with good luck during this fortunate period. Supportive relationships, an even flow of money, and happiness are yours. Do more. Put this time to constructive use in goal setting.

Jupiter-Moon: Your optimistic mood attracts pleasing, uplifting emotional contacts and experiences. Set aside plenty of time for your mate and other loved ones. Women can link you to opportunities.

Jupiter-Mercury: Communication, business deals, and studies benefit from your positive mindset. This is also an excellent time to sign contracts, network, travel near or far, and ask for favors.

Jupiter-Venus: It's easy to slip into a self-indulgent mode under this aspect. That's fine to a point. Everyone deserves lazy days. However, control your sweet tooth and set spending limits. Attract love.

Jupiter-Mars: Your high energy, drive, and confidence need a productive outlet. Focus them where you can realize maximum gain. This is also an excellent time to smooth over any lingering conflicts.

Jupiter-Jupiter: Life perks along, and it takes little effort to fulfill your desires. Use this easygoing phase to catch up with yourself, travel, learn, and socialize. Happy optimism attracts more of the same.

Jupiter-Saturn: Business success comes as a result of past efforts, and you find a happy medium between expansion and caution. Work and other responsibilities are easily met and exceeded.

Jupiter-Uranus: Sudden opportunities are a perfect match for your innovative ideas during a period of positive change. Take a class or travel to satisfy your need for mental stimulation. A windfall is possible.

Jupiter-Neptune: All is well as long as you don't ignore reality. This aspect can then put you in touch with your spiritual self. Get involved in a worthy cause that lives up to your ideals.

Jupiter-Pluto: Ambition is a driving force as you strive for success. Be a leader and inspire others to be the best they can be. Finances are in the black, but try to remember that you and your money are not invincible.

Jupiter-Ascendant: Personal and relationship happiness and optimism color your life. However, don't succumb to laziness. Use this time to develop your creative energy and to better your life and those around you.

Jupiter-Midheaven: You can get by with doing little now, but think twice before you do. This overall lucky period can advance your status if you exert effort. Use it to further your aims and to beautify your home space.

Saturn Transits

Saturn represents restriction, setbacks, and the past. It also rewards effort, responsibility, and playing by the rules. Saturn provides structure, the foundation on which to build long-term gains as well as life experience and lessons.

Saturn can frustrate as it teaches patience and gives lower vitality when your body needs rest more than action. Although it can take much of a lifetime to understand its rhythm, careful observation of its cycles can speed up the learning process.

Saturn moves through the entire zodiac about every twenty-eight years, forming action aspects to its natal place and to all other planets and angles in your chart every seven years. Reflect on events and your responses to previous contacts. Identify the common theme(s) so you're better prepared at the next Saturn transit. This review should give you a general idea of how you respond to Saturn, as well as ways to minimize its negative traits and capitalize on the positive ones.

In general, Saturn is the career planet and suggests delays, limitations, tough lessons, hard work, and older people. Saturn is also associated with security, authority, status, self-discipline, depression, patience, responsibility, achievement, restriction, and pessimism.

Saturn in the Houses

Saturn in the First House: Size up your strengths and weaknesses as you begin a multi-year process of self-evaluation. New personal directions begin to emerge as a result, although it's best to postpone starting new long-term endeavors.

Saturn in the Second House: Although this transit can limit income, it's not a given. Nevertheless, the thriftier you are, the better, which is one of two lessons of this transit. The other is values—deciding what's really important to you.

Saturn in the Third House: This time is excellent for long-term studies because it aids concentration. However, don't cut off communication, despite difficulties, especially with siblings and relatives. Taking time to think is beneficial; withdrawing is not.

Saturn in the Fourth House: Household and family changes are a given. Parental and childhood issues, domestic repairs, and relocation are common, but don't lock yourself into a big mortgage. Career changes are also possible since Saturn opposes the tenth house.

Saturn in the Fifth House: Children are more of a responsibility now and can limit your free time. Romantic interests are few, mostly because your attention is focused on practical creative projects. Avoid chancy investments and other financial risks.

Saturn in the Sixth House: You're in a period of hard work and increased responsibilities, but recognition is nearly nonexistent. Guard your health. It's easy to become rundown. Take time for you and to serve others. Volunteer efforts are rewarding.

Saturn in the Seventh House: People demand much of you and your time during this transit. Some relationships end; others are strengthened. Make each one a learning experience. If other factors are in synch, this can be a good time to marry.

Saturn in the Eighth House: Trim your budget and pay off debt rather than incurring more, regardless of your overall financial status. It's also smart to do an annual credit check and resolve discrepancies. Raises and inheritance depend on other current factors.

Saturn in the Ninth House: You're involved with business travel, in-laws, legal affairs, matters at a distance, or education as Saturn transits your ninth house. Learning is a priority, either as a teacher or a return to school to complete or begin a degree program.

Saturn in the Tenth House: This can be a career pinnacle or just the opposite. Live up to responsibilities and don't be tempted to take the easy way out. It will backfire. Relocation, primarily for business reasons, and parental concerns are possible.

Saturn in the Eleventh House: Accept a leadership position in an organization or group endeavor and learn delegation and teamwork. Friends help you redefine and achieve goals, and you can reconnect with people from the past or meet a soul mate.

Saturn in the Twelfth House: Time alone can be satisfying and productive. Use it to evaluate and learn from the past, as well as on a practical level to complete unfinished projects. Pay attention to your health and your body's signals. You need extra rest and sleep.

Saturn Action Aspects—Conjunction, Opposition, Square, Semisquare, Sesquisquare

Saturn-Sun: Work hard, finish what you start, and live up to your responsibilities. Although you won't see immediate rewards, the payback is down the road. Relationships can be trying, and you also feel tired. Rest and sleep as much as possible.

Saturn-Moon: Depression, loneliness, guilt, and isolation are common with these aspects. You feel isolated and without emotional support, which affects relationships and increases self-doubt. Try not to "give in" to the energy any more than necessary. Give yourself plenty of TLC.

Saturn-Mercury: Your thoughts drift to the negative and you can be overly concerned with details and critical of others. This hampers communication and can lead to disagreements. Condition yourself to replace pessimistic thoughts with upbeat ones. Welcome other viewpoints.

Saturn-Venus: Some relationships end; others are strengthened. The outcome depends in part on your attitude. You also could meet a soul mate during this time and gain increased partnership responsibilities. Learn to be thrifty if finances are tight.

Saturn-Mars: Frustration is your chief stressor now, which increases the potential for accidents and confrontations. Relieve tension and anger through mild exercise and learn to work within the established structure of your life.

Saturn-Jupiter: This period is one of learning experiences as you struggle with restrictions that make you crave freedom. Balance the desires as best you can. A job search is unlikely to produce results; protect your current position even though it's not ideal.

Saturn-Saturn: This aspect represents a turning point in your life as you review the past, face up to security and confidence issues, and look at how you deal with authority. It also can signal major achievements. Events now are usually tied to those of seven years before.

Saturn-Uranus: You have the urge to break free of perceived restrictions as your needs for security and independence conflict. Career and relationships are likely targets. Look for a happy medium, rather than wholesale change. Learn to live within the "rules."

Saturn-Neptune: Doubt and confusion add an unreal quality to life as stability fades and you debate reality versus the ideal. Career problems arise, and security dissipates. The best strategies are to find a creative or spiritual outlet and to protect your health.

Saturn-Pluto: This aspect, which signals endings, almost always produces major difficulties, such as financial trouble, a job layoff, power struggles, and control issues. Unfortunately, you feel powerless to fight back. Believe in yourself and move on. It may turn out to be a blessing in disguise.

Saturn-Ascendant: Relationships can be difficult; at the least, they require significant work. Those that should end will, and others will be strengthened. Loneliness and added personal responsibilities can drain your energy, so make sleep a priority, be open to change, and try to be patient with yourself and others.

Saturn-Midheaven: This is either a time of achievement or the exact opposite. Much depends upon the past and what you have earned. Review, revise, and move forward, no matter the outcome. Parents and other family members demand more of your time, as can household problems. Real estate purchases are usually unfavorable.

Saturn Background Aspects—Sextile, Trine, Conjunction

Saturn-Sun: Past efforts yield today's rewards. Take on additional tasks and set your sights on a promotion as you go out of your way to impress supervisors. Reap what you deserve.

Saturn-Moon: Emotions are steady, and you're attuned to family responsibilities. Use this phase to solidify your life foundation and set new career goals. It's also positive for real estate deals.

Saturn-Mercury: Communication, concentration, and clear, analytical thinking are your best assets now. Business benefits as long as you can detach from old habits and work methods. Expand your comfort zone.

Saturn-Venus: Relationships and money are stable, and important people favor you. If other factors are positive, this aspect is auspicious for marriage and business partnerships. Strengthen ties with loved ones.

Saturn-Mars: Slow, steady progress appeals to you, and hard work is as satisfying as it is productive. Even the most daunting tasks are no match for your determination. A to-do list is your best friend.

Saturn-Jupiter: Latch on to whatever career opportunities come your way. Be seen and heard by VIPs, and promote your aims. Further education is an excellent investment for future gains.

Saturn-Saturn: You feel secure and on track with your life and career. But give your goals a check-up. Revise them as necessary if you're in a holding pattern. Set your sights on the next short-term and long-term steps.

Saturn-Uranus: Welcome new opportunities that signal changes for the better. An unexpected job offer or promotion could come your way as people see your ability to blend the new with the old.

Saturn-Neptune: Set aside time for solitude and meditation. They help center you and invite new personal and professional insights. Create something concrete on your own or within your business.

Saturn-Pluto: You're focused, ambitious, and methodical as you strive to achieve. Ambitions are more easily realized now, but tread lightly. Lead by example and be a team player.

Saturn-Ascendant: Relationships are steady and dependable, and you are viewed as the same. Connect with people who can become mentors, and do the same for others.

Saturn-Midheaven: Your career goals are on track and you can realize them with the help of important people. But resist the temptation to fall into a rut. See beyond the present by building on the past.

Uranus Transits

Quirky Uranus brings the unexpected and change through internal and external events. Any attempt to predict its effects is futile. Although the outcome often seems obvious, it rarely is because Uranus sparks surprises and seems to delight in doing just the opposite. However, Uranus is a fairly accurate timer—events often occur when aspects are exact or within a few minutes.

An intuitive planet, Uranus energy is linked to flashes of insight, "light bulb" moments when what was previously unseen is suddenly apparent and fully understood. Be alert to these messages and follow up on hunches and chance encounters.

Whether subtle or overt, internal or external, Uranus signals change, a life circumstance that can be difficult during the best of times. Some people cope well with it; others fight it. Try to be open to change, especially during Uranus transits. Life will be easier, and you can benefit from the sense of freedom and independence that result.

Uranus is often involved when people seem to make sudden major decisions, such as divorce, marriage, and job/career changes. Although such events sometimes appear spontaneous to outsiders, the internal rumblings have been gathering momentum for some time. Retrograde patterns are often the key to timing, with the second or third contact producing action.

Uranus transits the zodiac every eighty-four years, moving through a sign/house in approximately seven years. The conjunction, squares, and opposition signal life-turning points.

Uranus in the Houses

Uranus in the First House: Your mission is to break free and redefine yourself. Become the "real" you, without the inhibitions of the past as you discover your independence. Be careful what you "toss out," though, including relationships. The changes are permanent.

Uranus in the Second House: Unexpected income can offset sudden expenses, but don't count on it. Build a nest egg and guard valuables against loss. A change in sources of income also is possible, such as a new job/career, second job, or sideline home-based business.

Uranus in the Third House: Open your mind to new attitudes, new information, and innovative ideas. Take classes, communicate, and expect the unexpected to govern daily life. Unusual events and group activities involve siblings, relatives, and neighbors.

Uranus in the Fourth House: Relocation, renovation, and other major domestic changes are likely. You can break free of old childhood influences and assert your independence by literally or figuratively separating yourself from family. Career changes are also possible.

Uranus in the Fifth House: This can be one of the most highly creative periods of your life. Find an outlet in anything from writing to crafts to painting. Pregnancy or sudden romance can catch you by surprise. Children test their independence.

Uranus in the Sixth House: Unexpected events can trigger a job change, or you can initiate it to find a more stimulating position or one that allows more freedom. It's important to move on if you feel stifled because such conditions can affect your health.

Uranus in the Seventh House: Relationships undergo a period of change, in part because of your need for excitement, which can spark an affair. Separation and divorce are possible, or you could elope. Try to restrain yourself until Uranus' influence is past.

Uranus in the Eighth House: Whether a windfall or loss, look for sudden financial developments, including an inheritance. Joint resources can be affected as a result of an income shift for you or your spouse. Avoid loans and credit, and stash cash for emergencies.

Uranus in the Ninth House: The world beckons you. Explore it in person or via books, TV, and the Internet. Further your education by traditional means or online, or study metaphysics and travel. Legal matters can be disruptive; avoid initiating lawsuits.

Uranus in the Tenth House: Your career and status are subject to change. Cover your bases and remain alert to a potential layoff or company bankruptcy. Begin a search if your current career/job feels restrictive; it's preferable to letting the boss make the decision for you.

Uranus in the Eleventh House: Group activities, clubs, organizations, and good causes interest you. They're an excellent source of new friends and contacts, which you're open to now. Many of them can influence your changing goals and be the links to opportunity.

Uranus in the Twelfth House: Secrets you thought safe are revealed, and other hidden factors come to light. Tune in to your sixth sense. It's on target, and your subconscious releases sudden insights. Program downtime to protect your health; nervous tension is high.

Uranus Action Aspects—Conjunction, Opposition, Square, Semisquare, Sesquisquare

Uranus-Sun: Free yourself to be the real you. If you think you've already achieved this status, take a deeper look. Let your solar energy shine through. This can be an exciting period of change in your life. Use exercise or other methods to relieve tension and stress.

Uranus-Moon: Expect emotional upsets, mood changes, and generally fluctuating emotions. Domestic changes are also possible, including relocation, electrical and appliance repairs, and people moving in or out. Carelessness can spark accidents.

Uranus-Mercury: Bright ideas, flashes of insight, and sudden news accompany this transit, which signals innovative thinking. But impulsiveness, snap decisions, and nervous tension can be your downfall. Intuition can be an asset if you take time to confirm it.

Uranus-Venus: Relationships begin and end suddenly under this transit, which also can spark love at first sight. Don't elope! It probably won't last. Existing relationships can benefit from positive change if you and your mate are open to it. Finances can go either way, up or down.

Uranus-Mars: You're impulsive, short-tempered, and prone to angry outbursts. The root cause is an attempt to assert your individuality. Try to direct the energy in a more positive way that stimulates personal growth. But be cautious about taking risks; they can lead to accidents.

Uranus-Jupiter: Seize opportunities if they're the real thing. It can be tough to know the difference now, so go easy and protect your resources. This transit also boosts your confidence. That's great as long as you don't view yourself as invincible. Use caution and common sense.

Uranus-Saturn: Many of the constants in your life are subject to change. Move past restrictions and let go of what you no longer need. Be cautious in career matters, however. Stick with it and work around difficulties. A new position is unlikely to last or satisfy you.

Uranus-Uranus: One way or another, your quest for independence marks this period as one that can send you in positive new directions—or just the opposite. Try to hang on to your common sense, and seek positive outlets to satisfy the urge to be different as you grow into your new self.

Uranus-Neptune: This transit can be enlightening if you don't succumb to illusion and the confusion that surrounds changing conditions. Question what's real and what's not. Drugs and alcohol can be a problem for you or someone close if such a tendency exists.

Uranus-Pluto: External change prompts internal change, which requires you to adapt. Take yourself in an entirely different direction or one that's an offshoot of current activities. Look for emerging opportunities and get in on the ground floor.

Uranus-Ascendant: The only constant in your life is change. Make it positive, and be true to yourself and your growing independence without tossing out your life. Be cautious in relationships. Don't sever or begin a partnership on a whim.

Uranus-Midheaven: A job/career change is as likely as relocation, significant home remodeling, or people moving in or out. Reevaluate your career goals. Stick with them if they're viable; if not, explore a new direction. A sudden layoff is possible.

Uranus Background Aspects—Sextile, Trine, Conjunction

Uranus-Sun: Connect with friends and groups. They add excitement and new experiences to your life. You also find self-expression easier in the sense that you're more comfortable with the real you, your solar energy.

Uranus-Moon: Meet people and make new friends. One could become a romantic interest. This is also the time to make positive relationship changes and to freely express your emotions. Listen to hunches.

Uranus-Mercury: You're curious, open to new ideas and creating plenty of your own, thanks to an active imagination. Take a class, or learn a new skill or hobby. It provides a nice break from your fast-paced daily life.

Uranus-Venus: Friends increase your luck and can be the catalyst for a windfall or romance. Socialize, but go beyond the same old places and activities. Go for what's new and different, and seek out interesting people.

Uranus-Mars: Energy is high, but keep tabs on your nervous tension. Relieve stress through exercise and spontaneous fun. You shine as a leader, so make your mark. Add a unique touch to all you do.

Uranus-Jupiter: Learn, grow, and add some sparkle and excitement to your life during this lucky period. Travel, teaching, and study are excellent avenues, whether for pleasure or to boost your marketable skills.

Uranus-Saturn: Your most effective course of action is to work for change within existing structures. Originality is a plus and one that gets you noticed on the job. Be a team leader. Relocation is also possible.

Uranus-Uranus: Take time for you, including outings with friends. This strengthens your independence and frees you from the daily grind. Share your talents in behalf of a humanitarian effort.

Uranus-Neptune: Charitable causes attract your attention. Be a hands-on volunteer. It feels good and has the side benefit of widening your circle of friends. Learn meditation techniques to enhance your intuition.

Uranus-Pluto: Expect far-reaching change to touch your life, mostly on an internal level. Your shift in perspective can come through other people or the study of metaphysics. New knowledge adds depth.

Uranus-Ascendant: Satisfy your need for independence through personal growth and change. Learn more about yourself and your relationships, and reap the benefits of both. Meet new people and develop your creativity.

Uranus-Midheaven: Initiate career changes, either in your current profession or a new one. Use your imagination, be innovative, and emphasize teamwork. Network through groups and friends.

Neptune Transits

Neptune, the planet of illusion, confusion, and deception, is also inspirational, creative, spiritual, and romantic. Sorting out what's what with Neptune can be a challenge if you're under its influence, and almost a snap if you're not.

When Neptune is active, you see what you want to see and hear what you want to hear. Reality is the furthest thing from your mind. Depending upon current circumstances, this can be a plus or a minus. It's marvelous for creativity, but dangerous for finances and in matters of the heart.

Neptune is also associated with water, chemicals, substance abuse, and medication. These problems occur more often with hard aspects, but not always. Difficult career aspects in combination with, for example, a progressed Mars-Neptune trine can suggest alcoholism as the root cause of a job loss. Just as easily, however, this can manifest as job disillusionment, creative vision, or co-worker deception.

Neptune moves so slowly through the zodiac that you are unlikely to experience any aspect beyond the opposition, which doesn't occur until you are in your mid 80s.

Neptune in the Houses

Neptune in the First House: You question your identity, who you are and what you want. Don't hurry the process. Give yourself time to evolve in tune with this new energy. Expect false starts and reversed decisions as you search for a new direction.

Neptune in the Second House: Avoid major financial decisions and risks, such as investments. Even in day-to-day transactions, money can slip through your fingers. Have faith that what you need will come, and reassess the value you place on material objects.

Neptune in the Third House: Misunderstandings occur frequently, and you easily slip into daydreams and wishful thinking. However, you're also attuned to the unseen and are sensitive to others. Inspiration comes through poetry, art, and music. Contracts can be misleading.

Neptune in the Fourth House: Family affairs are confusing, and straight answers are rare. Look beneath the surface. Also take precautions to avoid water-related problems, and use caution in real estate purchases. Home decorating benefits from this transit.

Neptune in the Fifth House: You attract romance and are idealistic in love. Protect your heart and your resources. This is a poor time for investment decisions, but excellent for creative endeavors. If you're a parent, keep a watchful eye on your children.

Neptune in the Sixth House: Health diagnoses are often difficult to make under this transit, and you can be sensitive to medication. Job disillusionment can drag you down, so fill the gap with creative pursuits and service projects until you can make a move.

Neptune in the Seventh House: Connections with others are blurred. Love captures your heart, but is it real or a false ideal? Business partnerships and professional contacts suffer from the same illusions. Drugs or alcohol can be part of the picture.

Neptune in the Eighth House: You can be a victim of fraud or misunderstanding in money matters. Check your credit report, and don't assume you and your partner are in financial synch. This is an excellent time to study metaphysics and to develop your intuition.

Neptune in the Ninth House: You seek answers to life's big questions as an interest in faith and spirituality triggers your quest. Travel, study, and dreams help reshape your attitudes, and you discover new creative outlets, such as photography and writing.

Neptune in the Tenth House: Career dissatisfaction begins to nag, but the solution remains illusive. Let it evolve naturally. In the meantime, keep close tabs on your current situation. Reality may be far different from what you observe and hear.

Neptune in the Eleventh House: Choose your friends and group activities wisely. Well intentioned or not, both can drain your energy and resources. Some inspire new goals, but others disappoint or deceive you. Protect yourself, but live up to the ideals of friendship.

Neptune in the Twelfth House: Solitude is beneficial as long as you don't withdraw from the world. Center yourself through daily meditation, which also opens your intuitive channels to the power of visualization. Use it to heal your spirit, to let go of what holds you back.

Neptune Action Aspects—Conjunction, Opposition, Square, Semisquare, Sesquisquare

Neptune-Sun: You question your life's direction and experience some confusion about what and who you are. Be careful of deception, initiated by you or someone else. Disappointment and disillusionment can come in the same package. Creativity and psychic ability are the advantages.

Neptune-Moon: Emotions are confusing, and this aspect often generates moodiness and tears. You're very sensitive now, so protect yourself from negative psychic energy; it can affect you in unseen ways. Domestic water problems are possible.

Neptune-Mercury: Major decisions are difficult because your thinking is fuzzy. Avoid them, and don't sign contracts. Misunderstandings are common, and someone who appears to be well-intentioned could deceive you. Indulge yourself in daydreams.

Neptune-Venus: The ultimate romance aspect, this duo also enhances your creativity and imagination. Try not to idealize love, however. Disappointment is the probable result, or you could fall into the trap of trying to "save" someone, such as an alcoholic.

Neptune-Mars: Your energy and efforts are diluted, so this is not the time to begin anything new. You also could become a scapegoat or unknowingly fall prey to an underhanded scheme. Replenish yourself with plenty of rest and sleep.

Neptune-Jupiter: You're idealistic and prone to false hopes and promises. As much as you want to help others, do it with caution. Some may try to take advantage of your good will. Satisfy the need by donating your time and talents to an established charity.

Neptune-Saturn: It's easy to slip into a pattern of self-doubt and worry when security diminishes. The structures in your life, such as career, relationships, and family, can be affected. Use recreational activities and hobbies to bolster your confidence and help take the edge off job disillusionment.

Neptune-Neptune: An uneasy feeling of dissatisfaction begins to surface in your life. It's as tough to get a handle on the problem as the solution. Let matters take their natural course; tap into your creative juices and wait it out. Answers eventually begin to emerge.

Neptune-Uranus: This transit activates your sixth sense, leading to fresh insights about life and your role in the world at large. This is not the time to stretch the truth or to entrust friends or groups with secrets. Sooner or later, they will be revealed.

Neptune-Pluto: Change is baffling, and the more you try to understand it, the less you succeed. This is, in part, because powerful people—possibly hidden enemies—try to undermine your efforts and mislead you. Be wary of forming alliances; cover yourself.

Neptune-Ascendant: Relationships are confusing, but no more so than your personal life, which feels directionless. Guard against those who would take advantage of you, but do become involved in a spiritual or charitable cause with ethical aims.

Neptune-Midheaven: Expect a growing sense of career dissatisfaction, but take no action until a new direction begins to emerge. Do the same with family, and burn no bridges. This is a poor time to purchase property, and you could encounter household problems related to water or chemicals.

Neptune Background Aspects—Sextile, Trine, Conjunction

Neptune-Sun: This is a peaceful, spiritual time in your life, and you're receptive to the needs of others. Music aids visualization, which can turn your daydreams and fantasies into reality.

Neptune-Moon: You're sensitive to the vibes of people and events as this aspect increases your sixth sense. Protect yourself from negative energy; absorb all that's positive and share the same with loved ones.

Neptune-Mercury: Intuition, imagination, and creativity add up to a unique combination that helps you sense what people are trying to say. It also aids you in learning, almost by osmosis. Take classes, or begin a journal.

Neptune-Venus: Love is lovely and so is romance. Enjoy them even if you have an idealistic view. Count your pennies. Money can evaporate with nothing to show for it. Be cautious with investments.

Neptune-Mars: This isn't the best time for new endeavors. It's better to maintain the status quo because your worldly ambitions are low. Reorient yourself to the softer side of life. Take it easy for a change.

Neptune-Jupiter: High hopes guide you. That's great as long as you accurately assess the risks involved in any undertaking. Get lost in romance, travel, learn a new hobby, or help those most deserving.

Neptune-Saturn: Envision a new reality, one that incorporates your most idealistic side with your practical one. Make the necessary sacrifices to achieve your aims, and inspire others by sharing your knowledge.

Neptune-Uranus: Whether you touch one person or thousands, make a difference in someone's life. Be there for a friend in need or get involved with a charitable or metaphysical organization.

Neptune-Neptune: Enrich your life in ways you've never before encountered. Explore your ideals, and determine what works and what doesn't. Find new truths that increase your world view.

Neptune-Pluto: Tap into your subconscious. Learn what makes you tick as you explore hidden urges. Don't be surprised if you discover unknown talents just waiting to be revealed. Use them to advantage.

Neptune-Ascendant: Form new relationships as long as they're based in reality and not idealism. Then you have much to offer each other and can benefit from the tie. A creative pursuit can open your intuitive side.

Neptune-Midheaven: Although your inclination now is to drift along and maintain the status quo at home and on the job, be alert to undercurrents. Meditation is one way to tune in; your sixth sense is another.

Pluto Transits

Pluto goes beyond mere change to another level—transformation. It challenges any planet or angle it contacts to move beyond events and into their core meaning. Out of understanding comes transformation, the process that replaces old, outworn structures with new, viable ones.

Pluto represents power, obsession, and events beyond your control, such as job layoffs and natural and manmade disasters. It also can signify Plutonian people in your life. Control freaks—those who manifest Pluto's energy negatively—are usually easy to spot. Positive Plutonians can be more difficult to identify because they are the catalysts who work subtly as agents for change.

Pluto moves so slowly through the zodiac—two to three degrees a year—that it will transit half or less of your chart in your lifetime. The years when it forms action aspects to your natal and progressed planets and angles are memorable for their intensity and sweeping change. As is true with the other outer planet transits, your willingness to work with the planetary energy can spell the difference between success and failure. The more you fight it—and in the case of Pluto, try to control it—the more difficult conditions become.

You may begin to feel Pluto's influence when the aspect is as many as three to four degrees from exact, and only rarely will an event occur when it is exact. In a sense, because of its slow movement, it forms the backdrop for the changing conditions that precede and ultimately bring about the transformation process. Other outer planet transits and progressions fill in the lessons and provide more specific details about what the Pluto transit signifies.

For example, in the case of a job layoff, the transformative issues involved could be security, limited education, or family responsibilities. These are the issues the individual must deal with; the actual layoff—the event—is the mechanism to initiate the transformation process. Such knowledge can be very valuable as the cycle unfolds. On a practical level, steps toward resolution will invite new—transformed—energy that will benefit the ensuing job search.

Pluto in the Houses

Pluto in the First House: A strong will gives you the power to make things happen. Use it wisely and for your own gain rather than through manipulation or control of others. Confidence grows as you test your personal limits in search of a new you.

Pluto in the Second House: Clean out junk and clutter. Learn what's important to you. A change in income reinforces this value-based message. Extend it beyond the things in your life to your personal philosophy and self-worth. Make the changes that define a new image.

Pluto in the Third House: Deep thinking characterizes this transit, which is positive and useful in exploring psychological motivations. However, try to maintain objectivity and an open mind. Relatives can be manipulative as they attempt to pressure you with guilt.

Pluto in the Fourth House: Change centers on home and family. Relocation, remodeling, or major repairs are likely, and parents or other relatives can be a concern. Divorce is possible. This is an excellent time to resolve childhood issues through counseling.

Pluto in the Fifth House: Love matches can be intense, obsessive, or both, and turmoil often ends dating relationships. Creative projects and exercise are good stress relievers, but avoid extreme sports. If you're a parent, expect children to test your limits and theirs.

Pluto in the Sixth House: Job conflicts and power struggles with supervisors and co-workers can prompt you to fight back. Don't. It's unwise to burn bridges; this transit can change your employment status. Do something positive for yourself. Live a healthy lifestyle.

Pluto in the Seventh House: Relationship tension builds as old resentments surface. Divorce is often the result, and other close ties are severed. Avoid entering into any partnership as Pluto crosses your Descendant or makes difficult aspects from the seventh house.

Pluto in the Eighth House: Although the process can be painful, use this transit to consolidate and pay off debt. If you're debt-free, keep it up and avoid risk. Finances can change at any time, for better or worse, depending upon other factors, most of which are out of your control.

Pluto in the Ninth House: Religion and spirituality may take on added importance as you search for in-depth knowledge and understanding. Higher education fulfills the same goal. Legal problems can develop during this time. Seek competent advice.

Pluto in the Tenth House: Your career reaches a pinnacle as Pluto transits the Midheaven. Use your drive and ambition to succeed—without stepping on toes. Conversely, you can be the victim of power plays or lose what you have spent many years achieving.

Pluto in the Eleventh House: Transformation comes through friends and groups, but be cautious. Align yourself with people who can be a force for positive change, rather than the opposite. The risk here is that you can become consumed by a cause.

Pluto in the Twelfth House: Your subconscious releases long-buried memories as Pluto urges you to resolve life issues. Work through them with therapy or a self-help group. Tune in to your sixth sense, which also offers valuables clues. Live a healthy lifestyle and get a check-up.

Pluto Action Aspects—Conjunction, Opposition, Square, Semisquare, Sesquisquare

Pluto-Sun: Drive and ambition can bring success, but also power struggles with those who perceive you as a threat to their own aims. Fairness, compromise, and teamwork ease most situations. Develop your leadership skills, and learn to handle conflict tactfully.

Pluto-Moon: Intense emotions, relationship changes, and subconscious urges upset your equilibrium. Try to separate fact from emotion to loosen the grip of your feelings, as difficult as it is. Relocation and household repairs may be needed. Clean out clutter and junk.

Pluto-Mercury: This aspect can manifest as conflict with authority figures, manipulation, and obsessive thinking. It also can reflect depression. At its best, this lineup is excellent for research, study, deep thinking, and persuasive communication.

Pluto-Venus: Some relationships reach a crisis point as stresses and strains, jealousy, and possessiveness surface. The most difficult are likely to end; others are transformed. You may be attracted to people who are married or otherwise unavailable.

Pluto-Mars: This time frame is one of major success or failure. Although your drive and determination are high, don't cross the line into ruthlessness. Sidestep power plays and protect your interests. Resist the temptation to push yourself too hard; physical injury could result.

Pluto-Jupiter: Ambition promises success or just the opposite if you take on more than you can deliver. Keep your limits in perspective even though you're optimistic. This transit can also signal legal problems and a domineering, self-righteous attitude.

Pluto-Saturn: The more you hang on to the past and existing structures, the more difficult change becomes. Let go and move on. Embrace personal and professional growth. The accompanying financial downturn, if it occurs, can be the result of a layoff or company restructuring.

Pluto-Uranus: You're in the mood to toss out those elements of your life that no longer work. Stop! Wholesale change is rarely a good idea, especially when it's prompted by the need to rebel against authority. Sort through your issues and examine them carefully.

Pluto-Neptune: Your world is changing in the global context, as it is for most people born in your generation. Keep an open mind and adapt to it. Gain understanding through metaphysical studies and by developing your spiritual foundation.

Pluto-Pluto: This aspect prompts you to examine your basic wants and needs, your power and effectiveness in the world and how you deal with authority and conflict. Take the initiative to revamp your approach, if necessary. Then others are less likely to force the issue.

Pluto-Ascendant: You're changing as much as the relationships in your life, and one has a significant impact on the other. Delve into your subconscious, and explore power issues—your own or those directed toward you—and other long-overdue personal changes.

Pluto-Midheaven: Whether by choice or as the result of a layoff or similar event, now is the time to revamp your career goals. Take care not to step on toes, however, because that can prevent you from achieving needed or desired change.

Pluto Background Aspects—Sextile, Trine, Conjunction

Pluto-Sun: You have the power to make things happen. Focus it on yourself and make self-improvement your main objective. It's also an excellent time for personal and career achievements.

Pluto-Moon: Connect with your emotions and rid yourself of psychological baggage. Clean out your physical house too. Remodel, renovate, or clear away years of clutter. This frees your space as much as your feelings.

Pluto-Mercury: This aspect is an asset in research as well as serious study. It also gives you insight into human nature, which teaches you more about yourself. Communication is powerful, yet positive. Speak in public.

Pluto-Venus: Love is intense, so much so that it generates the deepest of feelings. This benefits new and established relationships. Finances also benefit from this aspect, which helps you attract money.

Pluto-Mars: High energy, drive, and ambition propel you toward new successes, possibly the best of your life. Use your power wisely. Do something for yourself too. Exercise, eat right, and get in shape.

Pluto-Jupiter: Luck allows you to achieve more without expending maximum effort. Legal and financial affairs also profit from this aspect, and confidence is high because you believe in yourself.

Pluto-Saturn: Determination and staying power aid your every endeavor and help you rise above others who are less industrious. Thrift and caution help you make the most of personal and financial resources.

Pluto-Uranus: Move out of your usual world. Seek mental stimulation from new people, new ideas, and new experiences. They can have a profound effect on you and your psyche in subtle yet effective ways.

Pluto-Neptune: Examine your spiritual beliefs. Find out what works and what doesn't and incorporate the new insights into your everyday life. The study of metaphysics adds additional depth.

Pluto-Pluto: Subconscious urgings prompt subtle changes that ultimately can have a major impact on your life direction. Listen to them and fit them into your current framework as additional building blocks.

Pluto-Ascendant: Desired personal and relationship changes come easily now, and both you and your partner benefit from them. You're also drawn to powerful people who can help shape you for new directions.

Pluto-Midheaven: Whether seen or unseen, important people support you and your career interests. Aim for the top and a position where you can do the same for others, as you develop stronger ties with family.

8
Inner Planet Transits

Inner planets are triggers. They activate eclipses, progressions, and outer planet transits. The new and full Moons function in much the same way. The influence of a new Moon lasts about a month, until the next new Moon; it initiates events. The full Moon brings matters to conclusion in the two-week period that ends with the next new Moon.

Using an orb of one to two degrees, look for progressed and natal planets and angles aspected by the new or full Moon. Then note the house position of the new or full Moon and the progressed or natal planet or angle it aspects. (Aspects to natal planets generally have more impact than those to progressed planets.) The two in combination reflect the sphere of activity for the four weeks ahead.

For example, a second-house new Moon would target money. If it were to square a planet in the fifth house, you might have extra expenses related to children or win a game of chance, both of which are ruled by the fifth house.

An interesting phenomenon of the new and full Moons is an added help in predicting events. The new and full Moons are at the same degree from October/November through March/April every year. Only the sign changes. As a result, events begun in the fall evolve through the winter and into early spring as each succeeding new or full Moon aspects a planet/angle in a chart.

In general, the transiting Sun represents you and your sphere of activity; it can also represent men and authority figures, such as a supervisor. Mercury is communication, short trips, relatives, and younger people. Venus rules money, gifts, love, and relationships; it also symbolizes people and things that you desire and that attract you. Mars is action, energy, initiative, and men; it usually acts early (use a two-degree orb to be safe) and is active when accidents occur.

The Moon, which rules emotions and women, is the fastest-moving planet. It transits a sign about every two-and-a-half days and all twelve signs about every twenty-eight days. Because of its speed, the Moon often functions as a trigger, setting off events indicated by the other planets.

Be aware of the transiting Moon's sign and house position. Its house position yields more information about the sphere of activity. The Moon's sign usually reveals the timing of an event. Watch for days when the Moon, by sign, forms action aspects with other planets that indicate a potential event.

The planetary positions listed here illustrate how the Moon can function as a trigger.

Day	Planet	Planet Degree and Sign	Moon Degree and Sign
1	Mars	10°09' Sagittarius	0°–15° Virgo
	Saturn	12°09' Pisces	
2	Mars	10°48' Sagittarius	15°–29° Virgo
	Saturn	12°09' Pisces	
3	Mars	11°26' Sagittarius	29° Virgo–14° Libra
	Saturn	12°09' Pisces	
4	Mars	12°05' Sagittarius	15°–28° Libra
	Saturn	12°08' Pisces	
5	Mars	12°43' Sagittarius	29° Libra–12° Scorpio
	Saturn	12°08' Pisces, stationary direct	

Mars is square Saturn on Day 4, but the Virgo Moon forms action aspects (square and opposition) to both Mars and Saturn on Day 1. The event is thus most likely to occur before Mars and Saturn form an exact square. Note also that Saturn is powerful because it is stationing to turn direct.

On Day 3, still prior to the exact Mars-Saturn square, the Libra Moon will sextile Mars. On Day 5, when Mars and Saturn are exactly square, the Moon is in Scorpio, where it will trine Saturn. Unlike the square, an action aspect, the sextile and trine are background aspects and less likely to trigger the event signaled by the Mars-Saturn square.

The easiest way to quickly identify background and action aspects (other than the semisquare and sesquisquare) is by sign element and mode. Signs in the same mode (cardinal, fixed, mutable) form square and opposition aspects to each other. Signs in the same element (fire, earth, air, water) are trine each other, and those in complementary elements are sextile (fire-air, earth-water). Conjunctions can, of course, occur in any sign.

Now let's look at how the new Moon and inner transiting planets triggered David's birth chart, progressions, and outer planet transits.

Career Path

Decision to Return to School—August 23, 1991

David announced his decision to return to school when he arrived home from work at about 5:00 PM on August 23, 1991 (chart 13). The actual moment of the decision is unavailable.

The idea to return to school probably came together within a few hours earlier that day as the transiting Aquarius Moon in David's eleventh house of goals squared the progressed Mercury-Mars-Ascendant stellium in Taurus. This powerful combination was also active in the progressed and transiting outer planet contacts: progressed Mercury (education) sesquisquare natal Midheaven (career); transiting Neptune in the tenth house of career square natal Ascendant; progressed Ascendant sextile natal Saturn (Midheaven ruler, career) and transiting Jupiter (in the third house of education); and Uranus in the tenth house sesquisquare the Taurus stellium.

The progressed and transiting Sun (ruler of the sixth house of work) were also involved. The transiting Sun (it had entered the sixth house earlier that day) squared progressed Sun and sesquisquared natal Ascendant. The transiting Sun thus triggered the progressed Sun-semisquare-natal Ascendant aspect and transiting Saturn's trine to the progressed Sun.

Transiting Mars opposed natal Saturn, an aspect that can be difficult and one that often signals a time of frustration. In David's chart, however, the opposition prompted

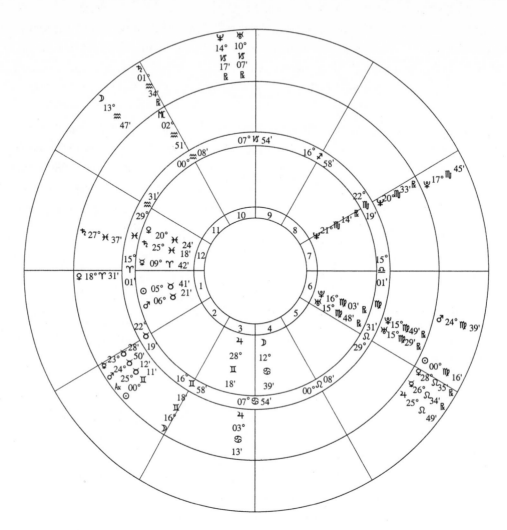

Chart 13

David's Progressed Chart with Transits

August 23, 1991 / Placidus Houses

Inner Wheel

Birth Chart

April 26, 1966

5:07 AM EDT

Middle Wheel

Progressed Chart

August 23, 1991

Outer Wheel

Transits

August 23, 1991

him to take career action. The tension of the opposition was eased by transiting action-oriented Mars trine the progressed Taurus stellium and transiting Saturn trine progressed Sun.

The necessary conditions were in place for David to take the initiative (Ascendant, Sun) to return to school (Mercury, Jupiter) to improve his status and career prospects (tenth house, Saturn) through a new job (Uranus-Pluto, Sun).

The event was initially energized by the August 9, 1991, new Moon at 17°00' Leo, which trined his natal Ascendant. The transiting inner planet aspects on August 23, 1991, were as follows:

- Transiting Sun square progressed Sun—Job motivation (Sun ruler of the sixth house)

- Transiting Sun sesquisquare/semisquare natal Ascendant/Descendant—Personal motivation for job action (Sun ruler of the sixth house)

- Transiting Mercury square progressed Mercury-Mars-Ascendant—The idea, snap decision, and initiative to return to school (Mercury ruler of the third house, Mars ruler of the Ascendant)

- Transiting Venus sextile natal Jupiter—Desire to attend school (Jupiter ruler of the ninth house)

- Transiting Mars opposition natal Saturn—Sudden career change (Mars ruler of the Ascendant, Saturn ruler of the tenth house)

- Transiting Mars trine progressed Mercury-Mars-Ascendant—Action related to job/school decision

Job Offer—December 12, 1995

David interviewed for the job on December 9, 1995, and received the offer by phone at 10:00 PM on December 12 (chart 14). His wife remembers the time because it was such an unusual hour for a job offer. In addition to transiting lunar aspects, the transiting Ascendant and Midheaven triggered the call.

Like the planets, the Ascendant and Midheaven move through the signs, transiting all 360 degrees of the zodiac each day. Their average motion is about four minutes per degree, two hours per sign. Both of these angles are thus in each sign for about two hours every day. Although the transiting Ascendant and Midheaven move too quickly to

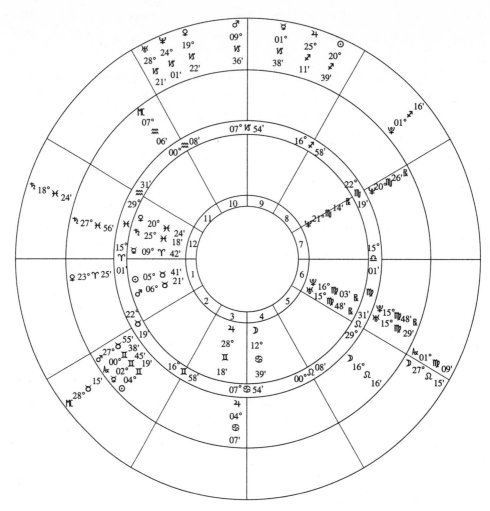

Chart 14
David's Progressed Chart with Transits
December 12, 1995 / Placidus Houses

Inner Wheel	**Middle Wheel**	**Outer Wheel**
Birth Chart	Progressed Chart	Transits
April 26, 1966	December 12, 1995	December 12, 1995
5:07 AM EDT		

be used in everyday forecasting, they can trigger an event, as in this example, but not without other indicators.

The November 22, 1995, new Moon at 29°52' Scorpio prompted David to go after what he wanted. It opposed the progressed Ascendant and Mars in the eighth and second houses of money. The full Moon of December 6, 1995, at 14°27' Gemini brought matters to conclusion as it sextiled the natal Ascendant and squared natal/progressed Uranus-Pluto in the sixth house of work.

The aspects that night were as follows:

- Transiting Sun square natal Venus—Job offer (Sun co-ruler of the fifth house, Venus ruler of the second and seventh houses)

- Transiting Moon square progressed Mars—Excitement, new beginning (Moon, emotions, and ruler of the fourth house), plus the job required relocation (Mars, action, and ruler of the Ascendant)

- Transiting Moon sextile natal Jupiter—Luck, communication (Jupiter in the third house)

- Transiting Mercury sesquisquare progressed Moon—Relocation news/job offer (Mercury in the ninth house, co-ruler of the sixth house; Moon ruler of the fourth house)

- Transiting Venus sextile natal Venus—Career/money/job offer (Venus in the tenth house, ruler of the second and seventh houses)

- Transiting Venus square progressed Neptune—Idealistic financial view (Venus ruler of the second house; Neptune in the tenth house)

- Transiting Mars square natal Mercury—Job offer (Mars ruler of Ascendant; Mercury ruler of the third house and co-ruler of the sixth house)

- Transiting Mars conjunct Midheaven (separating)—Career action (Mars, action, ruler of the Ascendant; Midheaven, career)

- Transiting Ascendant square progressed Ascendant and progressed Mercury—Job offer (Mercury ruler of the third house and co-ruler of the sixth house)

- Transiting Ascendant sesquisquare natal Ascendant—Self

- Transiting Midheaven conjunct progressed Mars—New career endeavor, personal success (Midheaven, career; Mars ruler of the Ascendant)

If David had asked you to study his chart once he had the interview date, you would have seen several auspicious aspects for December 9, 1995 (the interview date). A transiting Mercury-Jupiter conjunction that activated transiting Jupiter's square to natal Saturn, transiting Mars conjunct natal Midheaven, and transiting Venus trine natal/progressed Uranus-Pluto.

Seeing these aspects, you would have told him that he had a lucky and favorable opportunity (Venus and Jupiter) to sell himself (Mercury and Mars) to a prospective employer (Midheaven). After the interview, he would have asked you when he might receive an offer.

Mercury and the third house rule communication, such as a job offer, so the search begins there. As transiting Mercury separated from its conjunction with transiting Jupiter and its square to natal Saturn, it approached a square to progressed Saturn, the last aspect it would make to his chart before entering Capricorn. Although it's possible that the Mercury transit could bring a job offer, there were no other significant aspects from inner transiting planets to trigger the event.

However, looking forward a couple of days, transiting Mercury would sesquisquare progressed Moon at the same time that transiting Mars would square natal Mercury. This is a much stronger possibility because transiting Sun would be squaring natal Venus. Mars (self, ruler of the Ascendant) plus Mercury (communication, co-ruler of the sixth house) plus Sun (co-ruler of the sixth house) plus Venus (ruler of the second and seventh houses) equals a job offer.

But it also could have happened at any time that day because the three key transiting inner planets were within orb. Earlier, the transiting Leo Moon had squared the seventh-house (other people) natal/progressed Neptune, which would have "blocked" the offer. Shortly before, there was a transiting lunar-solar trine, which is a good illustration of how a background aspect usually does not spark an event. Had it been an action aspect, it might have triggered the square of transiting Sun and natal Venus. The transiting Moon's trine to progressed Venus had the same non-effect.

When the offer arrived, however, the transiting Moon was square progressed Mars and sextile natal Jupiter. At the same time, the transiting Ascendant and Midheaven were making aspects, triggering natal and progressed Ascendant, progressed Mercury, and progressed Mars, which was sextile progressed Saturn (natal Midheaven ruler) and in a trine with transiting Uranus (progressed Midheaven ruler). The transiting Midheaven was conjunct progressed Mars.

Although the transiting Midheaven and Ascendant would have been at approximately the same degrees a few days before and after December 12, it was the Moon at the right degree in combination with other inner planet transits that provided the confirming aspects for the phone call.

9
Inner Planet Transits, Houses, and Aspects

The inner planets have two functions: They spark minor events, such as a call from a friend, frustration, disagreements, or praise from the boss; and they act as triggers for long-term trends that signal major events.

Although the primary focus of the aspect write-ups in this chapter is minor events, you can use the information as a guide to interpret life's big events. The planetary energy is the same. The difference is that there are other factors to consider—progressions, outer transiting planets, eclipses, and new and full Moons—when predicting a wedding, promotion, windfall, or cross-country move (see chapter 8).

For example, progressed Mercury conjunct the IC suggests major changes on the home front—relocation, remodeling, or a family member moving in or out. Transiting Mercury conjunct the IC might prompt you to deal with accumulated paperwork and unread magazines.

In general, the squares, oppositions, conjunctions, semisquares, and sesquisquares create action. Trines and sextiles produce an easy flow of energy that can temper difficult aspects. Conjunctions can go either way, depending upon the planets involved (read both aspect sections, action and background). Whether positive or negative, conjunctions intensify the effect of the two planets. Overall, the Sun, Moon, Venus, and Jupiter have a more positive influence than do the other planets.

Sun Transits

Sun in the Houses

Sun in Aries/First House: The time is ripe for new endeavors, especially personal ones, because you're interested in fulfilling your own needs and desires. Confidence is high.

Sun in Taurus/Second House: Reassess your values, both material and personal. Clean closets, get organized, and update your look. Be conservative when shopping. Spend only what you can afford.

Sun in Gemini/Third House: The daily pace picks up, and you're on the go. Force yourself to take time out, even if only thirty minutes a day. Day or weekend trips are restful and relaxing.

Sun in Cancer/Fourth House: Home and family warm your heart, and you enjoy spending more time with both. Launch a home decorating or improvement project, or shop for a new place to call your own.

Sun in Leo/Fifth House: Your main interest is fun! Socialize, see a sporting event, romance a love interest, or get involved in creative projects and hobbies. But don't ignore your responsibilities.

Sun in Virgo/Sixth House: It's a great time for a lifestyle change. Get in shape, eat healthy, or volunteer your time and talents. Work incentive and productivity are high. Make the most of them.

Sun in Libra/Seventh House: Relationships and cooperative efforts color your life. Get in touch with people and form alliances. It's also a good time to consult experts and professionals.

Sun in Scorpio/Eighth House: Put your energy into money matters, including joint resources. Depending on other aspects, loans and other financial dealings can go either way. Be cautious.

Sun in Sagittarius/Ninth House: Expand your horizons on foot, by car, or by plane. Or learn through reading, the Internet, or TV. Expect contact from in-laws and other people at a distance.

Sun in Capricorn/Tenth House: Be a leader and present your best in front of the boss and important people. Career gains, including a promotion, are now possible. Touch base with your parents.

Sun in Aquarius/Eleventh House: Take a break. Arrange get-togethers with friends, and socialize and connect with like-minded groups. Networking opportunities open up new possibilities.

Sun in Pisces/Twelfth House: Retreat from your busy life through meditation and solitude. Access your sixth sense, but be alert for those who have less than your best interests at heart.

Sun Action Aspects—*Conjunction, Opposition, Square, Semisquare, Sesquisquare*

Sun-Sun: You are the center of your world. That's great as long as you keep your ego in check. Do that, and you can achieve with determination. But don't drive yourself to the max. Be kind to your mind and body.

Sun-Moon: Emotions drive you to succeed, but difficulties arise when your ego and feelings clash. Keep them in perspective and try to balance the two influences. Get in touch with your subconscious desires.

Sun-Mercury: Errands, calls, meetings, and mail keep you on the move. Throughout it all, your brain works overtime. Listen as much as you talk and be receptive to other ideas and opinions.

Sun-Venus: Relationships go well or just the opposite. It depends on your willingness to compromise. Share your affections, socialize, and meet new people, rather than slip into laziness. Control spending and sweets.

Sun-Mars: New endeavors work out well if you plan before you act. They're a good use of your high energy and drive, but slow the pace to avoid accidents and sidestep arguments.

Sun-Jupiter: Don't let optimism get the best of you. Deliver on promises made and take on only what you can complete. You make your own luck through solid effort and a realistic approach.

Sun-Saturn: Low energy accompanies delays and stumbling blocks, but continue to persevere, plan, and organize. You work best on your own now, away from those in authority who can spark conflict.

Sun-Uranus: An independent streak takes hold, prompting restlessness. Take a break, go for a walk, and accept restriction as a part of daily life. Adapt when the unexpected occurs; change is inevitable.

Sun-Neptune: Turn the urge to escape into a positive. Tap your creativity and listen to your intuition. Meditation is a good outlet if you're unsure what you want or what path to take. Get a good night's sleep.

Sun-Pluto: Power issues come to the forefront. Analyze your motives if you're the source of the issue, and steer clear of those who try to exert control. Be smart. Protect yourself from physical harm.

Sun-Ascendant: Take care not to alienate others as you pursue your own interests. Instead, view them as a mirror image of yourself. You might learn more than you thought possible about life and relationships.

Sun-Midheaven: Connect with important people who can advance your ambitions. But be subtle, and minimize your ego. Do the same with family. Put their needs on an equal footing with yours. Quality time counts.

Sun Background Aspects—Sextile, Trine, Conjunction

Sun-Sun: All goes smoothly under this positive influence, which is also great for socializing. Sports, hobbies, and ego-building activities are positive outlets that allow you to shine.

Sun-Moon: You feel and look good, and your friendly aura attracts people. Get acquainted. Host a small get-together for pals or enjoy leisurely hours with your family or best friend.

Sun-Mercury: Curiosity enhances your communication skills, which are an asset in meetings and interviews. Sign contracts, shop for and repair mechanical devices, and handle personal paperwork.

Sun-Venus: You're in a good mood and as affectionate as you are popular. Have dinner with your mate or a date and friends. This transit also benefits finances and business negotiations.

Sun-Mars: You zip through most anything you tackle, thanks to a high level of energy and confidence. Limit new projects, however, to increase the chance of finishing them. Exercise is refreshing.

Sun-Jupiter: A lucky streak is a winning combination with your enthusiastic optimism. You're in the right place at the right time. Plan a vacation or pack your bags and take off.

Sun-Saturn: Your strong work ethic equals high productivity and potential career gains. Apply for a job or promotion, compile a thorough to-do list, and make the most of your determination.

Sun-Uranus: Opt for the right environment, the one where you're free to be you in group activities and socializing with friends. Variety negates boredom, as does doing what you enjoy.

Sun-Neptune: Let intuition be your guide in sensing what others think and feel. Trust it until proved otherwise and offer a helping hand to those who need it. See a movie or crank up the music.

Sun-Pluto: Willpower is your number one resource. Use it wisely and profitably to make positive changes and to impress important people. First get organized by tossing out distracting junk and clutter.

Sun-Ascendant: Build relationships, both personal and professional, through social and business gatherings. It's mostly effortless because people respond to your vibes. In return, your needs are fulfilled.

Sun-Midheaven: Stretch yourself and your ambitions. Set new targets for achievement, and then lead by example. Praise results. Your family adds depth to your life. Tell them you care.

Moon Transits

Moon in the Signs and Houses

Moon in Aries/First House: Your emotional responses are quick and up-front. That's positive if you're sensitive and tactful. Others are then likely to respond with mutual caring and kindness.

Moon in Taurus/Second House: Resist the tendency to shop or eat to lift your spirits. Do something constructive instead. Bolster self-esteem by treating yourself well. Get a manicure and massage.

Moon in Gemini/Third House: Your thoughts and decisions are emotionally motivated. Keep that in mind; within a few days you could have a change of heart. Do share your feelings with relatives.

Moon in Cancer/Fourth House: You feel comfortable and secure at home, so try to spend more time there the next few days. Cook for fun, entertain, or enjoy rare quality time with your family.

Moon in Leo/Fifth House: Voice your love, whether for a friend, partner, or child. Play brings joy to your life, as does creating something heartfelt for your home or a family member.

Moon in Virgo/Sixth House: On a practical level, domestic chores are tiring but satisfying. Avoid the inclination to criticize those closest to you and to suffer in silence from hurt feelings.

Moon in Libra/Seventh House: You share an affectionate rapport with others, especially your partner and loved ones. If conflict arises, however, try to put your emotions on hold. People will sense this weak spot.

Moon in Scorpio/Eighth House: Emotional connections are intense, and you are possessive of people and things. Reverse this tendency. Clear out clutter, and sell or donate what you don't need.

Moon in Sagittarius/Ninth House: Smile, laugh, and be happy. See a comedy, spend time with lighthearted friends, or explore the wonders of nature. Reconnect with childhood or school friends.

Moon in Capricorn/Tenth House: Go "public." Be seen and heard by those who can further your aims, and do the same for others. Connections forged now will pay off in the long run.

Moon in Aquarius/Eleventh House: Act on your fond feelings for friends. Reach out to them—call, write, or get together. The emotional support they offer you is a blend of caring and good advice.

Moon in Pisces/Twelfth House: Listen to your intuition. It guides you in knowing who to trust with your deepest feelings and secrets. Protect yourself against negative energy. You're highly sensitive now.

Moon Action Aspects—Conjunction, Opposition, Square, Semisquare, Sesquisquare

Moon-Moon: Moodiness and deep feelings are a signal to get in touch with your emotions. Look at your reactions and habits to find the root causes. Doing so increases your sensitivity to others.

Moon-Mercury: Keep this in mind: Thoughts and decisions are emotionally based and subject to change. Talk about your feelings with someone who's objective and willing to spell out the facts. Listen and take the advice to heart to help avoid regrets.

Moon-Venus: Window-shop, but don't spend. Socialize, but don't overindulge. Moderation is best, except with those you love. Treat them to plenty of TLC, with no expectation of the same.

Moon-Mars: Your actions are based on emotion and therefore can be impulsive. Try to ignore petty annoyances; consider the source, quell your irritation, and move on. Reject negative vibes.

Moon-Jupiter: Optimism and a desire for freedom motivate you to move forward with confidence. Channel them into a constructive endeavor to curb impatience and welcome new views on life issues.

Moon-Saturn: Your mood drops as pessimism and the weight of responsibility take hold. Rely on yourself if needed support is missing, rather than feeling guilty or lonely. Find joy in something simple.

Moon-Uranus: You're restless and impulsive, as your emotions and moods fluctuate from one extreme to the other. Stimulate your mind, or go for a walk to ease the influence of your short attention span.

Moon-Neptune: You're sensitive to people and your environment. Be careful. Protect yourself from negative energy. Daydreams are a good escape valve for this sentimental phase. Listen to hunches.

Moon-Pluto: Intense feelings can prompt jealousy and possessiveness, as well as an emotional power struggle. Re-center, be calm and rational, and put worries in perspective, even if you feel powerless.

Moon-Ascendant: Communicate your feelings to those close to you. Offer them your assistance, care, and concern. This fulfills your need for emotional intimacy and builds mutual support.

Moon-Midheaven: Career and family pressures urge you to realign priorities. Fortunately, you easily sense what others want and need. Respond accordingly while satisfying your own desires.

Moon Background Aspects—Sextile, Trine, Conjunction

Moon-Moon: In both your public and private lives, you're in touch with your emotions and those of others. Family life is especially meaningful, and comfort food and cozy hours with loved ones re-center you.

Moon-Mercury: Get on the phone, send out snail and e-mail, and run domestic errands. Then settle in for a long chat with your best friend or a special relative. Express your heartfelt emotions.

Moon-Venus: A date, whether with your partner or someone new, gets a thumbs-up from this transit. So does a lazy time at home with loved ones. Beautify your space with a plant or flowers.

Moon-Mars: Your energy and confidence rub off on others, so generate action and take the lead in a small project. Share ownership and take time to bring others up to speed.

Moon-Jupiter: Your happy, easygoing mood prompts laughter and learning. Gain knowledge from everyone you talk with and leave each one with a smile. Soon you see the big picture.

Moon-Saturn: You feel secure, although reserved, and patience is helpful in dealing with minor challenges and unimaginative people. Whether a friend or relative, brighten an older person's day.

Moon-Uranus: Club meetings, group activities, and friends give you a lift and a pleasant surprise. Introduce yourself to new people; one of them could provide an unexpected link to someone else.

Moon-Neptune: Sentimental and sensitive, you have a soft spot for loved ones, close friends, and those in need. Offer support without taking on their baggage. Daydreams are a delightful diversion.

Moon-Pluto: Depth of emotion allows you to get in touch with your feelings. On a practical level, tend to domestic repairs and restore order. Clean closets and drawers to satisfy the urge for change.

Moon-Ascendant: Congenial relations with everyone from co-workers to partners make life pleasant. Smile, spread cheer, offer assistance to reinforce mutual support, and trade TLC with your mate.

Moon-Midheaven: Job visibility nets satisfaction and praise. Make it happen by being front and center. Be there for your family, too. Share your feelings during quiet moments that touch your heart.

Mercury Transits

Mercury in the Signs and Houses

Mercury in Aries/First House: Speak up and express yourself during this clearheaded, quick-thinking phase, but resist making snap decisions and retorts. If you're restless, take a walk to calm nervous energy.

Mercury in Taurus/Second House: Think and plan before you spend. Comparison shop, and read up on financial matters. It's good to be open to differing opinions, but don't compromise your values.

Mercury in Gemini/Third House: Errands, calls, mail, meetings, and appointments occupy more of your time. You easily find the information you seek, and neighbors are helpful.

Mercury in Cancer/Fourth House: Devote extra hours to your family. Share your thoughts and feelings. Hands-on domestic projects are rewarding. Take a class to learn do-it-yourself skills.

Mercury in Leo/Fifth House: Socialize, read for pleasure, see plays or movies, or create something with your hands or mind. Sporting events, games, and outings with children are entertaining.

Mercury in Virgo/Sixth House: Mental effort and details command your attention at work. Send out resumes if you're job hunting. Exercise, rest, and good food help counteract the effects of nervous tension.

Mercury in Libra/Seventh House: Contracts and negotiations benefit from this transit, which emphasizes compromise. Open communication strengthens relationship and partnership ties. Meet people.

Mercury in Scorpio/Eighth House: Include your partner in financial decisions; make them after thorough research and discussion. Probe your subconscious in private moments. Listen to hunches.

Mercury in Sagittarius/Ninth House: Teach, take a class, or learn on your own through books, casual conversation, and travel. People at a distance are an excellent source of information.

Mercury in Capricorn/Tenth House: Get better acquainted with the boss and offer to make presentations. Both can advance your aims. But try not to get bogged down with paperwork and calls.

Mercury in Aquarius/Eleventh House: Teamwork is your best avenue to success, and networking runs a close second. Socialize, and get involved in group activities. All offer good insight for new goals.

Mercury in Pisces/Twelfth House: You hear secrets, but don't share your own because someone is likely to reveal them. Take time to think, read, sleep, and meditate. A slower pace is good for you now.

Mercury Action Aspects—Conjunction, Opposition, Square, Semisquare, Sesquisquare

Mercury-Mercury: Life is hectic as people and errands consume your time and energy. Try to stay focused amid distractions to capitalize on your active mind. Take time to think things through.

Mercury-Venus: Take the initiative to resolve minor disagreements so they don't fester. Peace is easily achieved. Social events are a pleasant diversion. Mix, mingle, and get acquainted, but don't overeat.

Mercury-Mars: Strong mental energy generates ideas, but can also lead to snap decisions and angry outbursts. Make it a policy to think before you speak and act, and ease up on the gas pedal during this accident-prone period.

Mercury-Jupiter: Focus on the big picture, but not to the exclusion of important details. Be realistic about what you can complete in the allotted time. Optimism is great as long as you produce.

Mercury-Saturn: This aspect aids concentration, but it also brings out worries and regrets. Try not to dwell on them. Look to the future rather than the past, except as a learning experience, which is where the real benefit lies. Deal with your own responsibilities; leave the rest alone.

Mercury-Uranus: Innovative thinking is a plus, but avoid making impulsive decisions and comments. Be prepared to go with the flow. Unexpected news and developments require a change of plans.

Mercury-Neptune: Cover your bases. Confusion and misunderstandings are likely, and your thoughts are foggy. Keep secrets and rumors to yourself. The latter are based more in fiction than fact.

Mercury-Pluto: Find the fine line that divides intensity from obsession. Then you're ready for concentration, study, and research. Keep your distance from those with power issues, and don't push your opinions on others.

Mercury-Ascendant: Take time from your busy schedule to talk with your spouse or partner. This satisfies your need for mental stimulation as much as it strengthens ties and puts you on the same wavelength.

Mercury-Midheaven: You excel at presentations and public speaking, provided you keep an open mind. Do the same in meetings. You're likely to receive career and family news. Include loved ones in domestic planning.

Mercury Background Aspects—Sextile, Trine, Conjunction

Mercury-Mercury: Meetings, appointments, news, communication, and errands fill your time. Learn as you go, and pick up useful bits of trivia. Sign contracts and forge agreements if overall conditions are favorable.

Mercury-Venus: Occupy yourself with a hobby, take a day trip with friends, shop, or see a concert. Express your love for others, flirt, or welcome a new relationship. Your friendliness attracts people.

Mercury-Mars: You think quickly and instantly grasp the facts. That's a plus if you're in sales or simply want to sell yourself and your ideas in a meeting or interview. Let your inner confidence shine through.

Mercury-Jupiter: This transit is excellent for planning, teaching, travel, business, and legal matters. It also produces good news that reinforces your positive, upbeat mindset. Think big.

Mercury-Saturn: The strong points of this transit are planning and organization, along with the ability to concentrate and make decisions. Career gains are possible; learning is guaranteed. Pay attention to details.

Mercury-Uranus: Be spontaneous and trust your intuition when imagination produces innovative solutions. Teamwork leads to brainstorming, and you click with new and old friends, who offer mental stimulation.

Mercury-Neptune: Go beyond facts and common sense. Unleash your creative urges, which are far stronger, but shy away from important decisions. See a movie or get lost in a novel.

Mercury-Pluto: You see beyond the obvious and can easily solve puzzles and mysteries. Do research and study, but don't get so wrapped up in the task at hand that you lose sight of all else.

Mercury-Ascendant: Take a one-time class for fun or profit, or arrange a get-together with neighbors or siblings. In between, run personal errands, handle paperwork, and catch up with your mate.

Mercury-Midheaven: Make the most of this visible phase. Communicate, plan, speak, and finalize business deals. It's also great for interviews because you come across as one in the know.

Venus Transits

Venus in the Signs and Houses

Venus in Aries/First House: This is a sociable, fun-loving time. You attract people, and new love is possible. However, treat your body kindly. Enjoy life without over-indulging in sweets.

Venus in Taurus/Second House: Gifts and money come your way, and you could be in line for a pay raise. Stash extra cash before your desire for luxuries prompts a spending spree.

Venus in Gemini/Third House: Charm and tact are an advantage in talks and meetings, and you easily sell yourself and your ideas. Set aside a day or weekend for a quick trip with friends or your mate.

Venus in Cancer/Fourth House: Get comfy at home. It's your favorite place now. Beautify your space with plants, pillows, or a painting, and enjoy leisurely hours with family and friends.

Venus in Leo/Fifth House: Party, date, play, socialize, and have fun! Save time for romance, and get concert or theatre tickets. Creative urges are strong; use them to express your unique self and style.

Venus in Virgo/Sixth House: Your work life is as satisfying as are your relationships with colleagues. Make the most of a mutually supportive atmosphere to generate quality output. Watch your waistline!

Venus in Libra/Seventh House: This is an excellent time to resolve relationship difficulties and strengthen ties, trade favors, and consult professionals. Compromise helps negotiations.

Venus in Scorpio/Eighth House: Loans, investments, and major purchases are positive if other influences signal the same, and your partner could receive a windfall or salary increase. Save first and spend later.

Venus in Sagittarius/Ninth House: Take a first or second honeymoon, attend a reunion, or travel with friends. Learn, wherever you are. Knowledge gained now and contacts made soon come in handy.

Venus in Capricorn/Tenth House: You easily gain the boss's favor, which could lead to a promotion. A job search launched now can have a positive outcome. Seek favors from important or older people.

Venus in Aquarius/Eleventh House: Friends and socializing are a priority. Mix, mingle, and get acquainted. You could meet a new love interest or career contact. Set aside quality time for close pals.

Venus in Pisces/Twelfth House: Leisurely quiet hours with your mate are appealing, as is time alone to read and create. But also help others. Volunteer activities are particularly rewarding.

Venus Action Aspects—Conjunction, Opposition, Square, Semisquare, Sesquisquare

Venus-Venus: Pure pleasure attracts you, as does a get-together with friends, your mate, or a potential love interest. Compromise if minor relationship tensions emerge. Trade favors, and keep everyone happy.

Venus-Mars: You're in the mood for romance and socializing. Do both, but don't make snap decisions about a new relationship. Opt for passionate moments with your mate, rather than an argument.

Venus-Jupiter: Good cheer is a plus in relationships, and you also could receive a small windfall. Skip shopping, however. Expensive items are far too appealing. Sweets and rich foods fall in the same category.

Venus-Saturn: It's tough to connect with people, and you feel isolated. Take advantage of this time to get in touch with your feelings. Time helps understanding and eases or prevents strained relations.

Venus-Uranus: Relationships are either up or down, but not in-between. Love at first sight is as likely as the end of an unworkable partnership. But don't be too hasty to satisfy your thirst for independence and excitement.

Venus-Neptune: Romance captures your heart, and it's okay to idealize love as long as you're aware that perfection is an illusion. Money is a different matter. Avoid making major financial decisions, loans, and investments.

Venus-Pluto: Love and other relationships are heavy with jealousy and possessiveness. Ease up, or walk away from one who attempts to manipulate you. Refuse to be drawn into power plays.

Venus-Ascendant: Enjoy time with friends and loved ones, and meet someone new. Treat yourself to a small, inexpensive gift, and do the same for someone you love.

Venus-Midheaven: Your workplace popularity rises, but family relations require more effort. Combine them if possible by entertaining at home and mixing business with pleasure.

Venus Background Aspects—Sextile, Trine, Conjunction

Venus-Venus: Relationships, money, and your love life benefit from this transit, which also puts you in the mood for a concert, play, or arts and crafts project. Keep an eye out for gifts.

Venus-Mars: Make the first move if you feel the spark of attraction. Invite your romantic interest to a party or sporting event. Others also view you favorably, and they willingly respond to your requests.

Venus-Jupiter: Luck is with you in love and money, but it's still wise to hang on to your common sense. Leisurely social events are appealing if you're feeling lazy. That's okay, but don't overindulge.

Venus-Saturn: Make conservative investments for the long term and strive for similar gains in business, personal, and professional relationships. This transit is also favorable for property deals and domestic purchases.

Venus-Uranus: Make yourself available for love. It could arrive in the most unexpected way, complete with sizzle. New friendships click too, and you could receive a windfall or stumble onto a lucky find.

Venus-Neptune: Romance, soft music, daydreams, and fantasy are the ultimate. Live them with someone you love. Kind words and hugs bring joy to others, who appreciate your care and concern.

Venus-Pluto: Your subtle yet powerful charisma attracts people, and you experience the depths of love as relationship passion intensifies. Pull yourself away long enough to update finances and investments.

Venus-Ascendant: You're as pleasant as the people you meet. Trade favors and compliments, have fun, relax, and socialize. But keep tabs on sweets and fat calories. Both are tempting.

Venus-Midheaven: It takes little to impress the boss or a prospective employer; be your charming best. Add a touch of beauty to your home, host a party, or enjoy delightful hours with your family.

Mars Transits

Mars in the Signs and Houses

Mars in Aries/First House: Your activity level matches your high energy. That's great, but get enough sleep and don't push your limits. Accidents are possible. Take the lead at work and play, but go easy on others.

Mars in Taurus/Second House: Determination is high. Use it to clean out clutter and closets, rather than adding to it with a spending spree or impulse buys. Defend your beliefs, but keep an open mind.

Mars in Gemini/Third House: Think before you speak to avoid sparking an argument. Daily life is fast paced, but ease up on the gas pedal. This period has accident potential. Stretch your mind and learn.

Mars in Cancer/Fourth House: Work around the house, and take care of minor repairs. Family conflict is possible because actions are based on emotion. Express love rather than irritation. Be understanding.

Mars in Leo/Fifth House: You find pleasure in sports, sex, socializing, and hobbies, and prefer play to work. Be reliable; do both. Take care if you exercise. Strains and sprains are possible.

Mars in Virgo/Sixth House: You're in the mood to work hard and can meet all your objectives. Share the load when necessary. There's no need to do everything yourself. Healthy food and sleep restore energy.

Mars in Libra/Seventh House: Relationships suffer if you come on too strong. Focus on cooperation rather than conflict. Then you get the best from business and personal partnerships.

Mars in Scorpio/Eighth House: Avoid spur-of-the-moment loans and purchases. Make more money, link resources with your mate to reassess financial strategy, pay off debt, and reduce expenses.

Mars in Sagittarius/Ninth House: Be open to new insights and learn all you can during this period of quick mental activity. Pass knowledge on to others. Legal battles are possible; try to avoid them.

Mars in Capricorn/Tenth House: Go all out to advance your status and career, but take care not to step on toes. Doing so will negate gains, as will working solo. Polish your leadership skills.

Mars in Aquarius/Eleventh House: Add your energy to team projects and sports. You excel at both. Tread carefully with friends, though. A clash of egos could cause you to part ways.

Mars in Pisces/Twelfth House: Although you receive little recognition now for your efforts, forge ahead and sidestep roadblocks. Work on your own, if possible. Calm yourself through meditation.

Mars Action Aspects—Conjunction, Opposition, Square, Semisquare, Sesquisquare

Mars-Mars: High energy requires a physical outlet, but don't max yourself out. Accidents are possible. New endeavors are favorable if they're based on well thought-out plans. Curb your temper.

Mars-Jupiter: Strong drive and energy to achieve put you in high gear. Direct them carefully to avoid the pitfall of overconfidence. Although you're inclined to do so, this is not the time to take risks.

Mars-Saturn: Frustration, impatience, irritation, and anger can steer you off course. Deflect them through precise work that requires high concentration and little or no contact with those in authority.

Mars-Uranus: Impulsiveness can result in accidents. Slow down, and find an outlet for your rebellious mood. Do the same if anger threatens to get the best of you. Take no chances.

Mars-Neptune: It's difficult to focus, in part because your energy is low and you're unsure of yourself. Save new endeavors for another day. See a movie, read poetry, rest, relax, and sleep.

Mars-Pluto: Used properly, your drive and ambition are assets. Don't undermine your efforts by pushing others or coming on too strong to the boss. Doing so is likely to result in a power struggle.

Mars-Ascendant: You're edgy with bottled-up tension. Release it through mild physical activity rather than anger that's harmful to relationships. Be careful with knives and tools so you don't cut yourself.

Mars-Midheaven: Involve others in your activities even though it's easier to do things yourself. Otherwise, they might see you as a threat. Be quick to make amends if your personal and professional lives clash.

Mars Background Aspects—Sextile, Trine, Conjunction

Mars-Mars: High energy equals high output, and new ventures get off to a great start. Be a leader and make the most of your self-confidence. Burn off excess energy through exercise. Try herb tea to lull yourself to sleep.

Mars-Jupiter: Initiate or follow up on new opportunities with growth potential, and seek avenues for tactful self-promotion. Your enthusiastic optimism makes that an easy task.

Mars-Saturn: Set goals and achieve them through patient, persistent effort as you work around roadblocks. Such diligence impresses the powers that be and raises your status another notch.

Mars-Uranus: Restlessness prompts you to seek variety and change. That's great as long as you find constructive outlets. Be a group, club, or team leader, and seek out new people and physical activity.

Mars-Neptune: Take steps to make dreams come true even if they seem a bit hazy. Meditation and visualization help, as does stimulating your creativity and imagination. Dance, and listen to music.

Mars-Pluto: You're self-directed and motivated as your inner drive comes alive. Let it take you where you want to go, but also look inward. Look for clues to why you react the way you do.

Mars-Ascendant: This transit is excellent for physical work, sports, and exercise. Just take care not to push your limits. Other personal activities are equally successful because you're highly charged.

Mars-Midheaven: Fulfill your ambitions. Go after exactly what you want career-wise. Do the same on the home front. Begin renovations, house hunt, or relocate. But be cautious with tools and heavy objects.

10
Relationships

People and relationships characterize much of life. They range from casual passing acquaintances to those that are lifelong. And love takes many forms—romance, friendship, family.

The most intense, personal, and influential relationships—whether ultimately positive or negative—are those that bring two people together in a romantic partnership. Personal chemistry both attracts and repels. It defines individual perception of the ideal mate. Love clicks when the timing is right, and clashes when it isn't.

Some people fall in love with love itself many times over; others fall in love only a few times before settling on a lifetime partner. Such tendencies, as well as the overall approach to relationships and the strengths and weaknesses brought to each one, are reflected in the natal chart.

Keep this in mind as you search for the right time, the right opportunity, to find love and romance. For example, someone with a natal Venus-Saturn aspect is less likely to leap into a relationship than someone who has a natal Venus-Uranus aspect. The first would be more cautious, the second more likely to fall in and out of love many times over. Another person with a Venus-Neptune conjunction would search eternally for the "perfect" mate.

Whatever the natal configuration, the predictive factors that indicate romantic opportunities—or the opposite—are constants. From there, it's a matter of free will and what the individual chooses to do with the progressions and transits. Sometimes the aspects that indicate commitment are closely followed by those that show conflict, as you will see in the example of the short-lived marriage of Marilyn Monroe and Joe DiMaggio. It's therefore a smart idea to look ahead a year or two when contemplating marriage.

Listed here are the aspect configurations present at the time of marriage or commitment. Each component must be "active"; that is, each appropriate planet and angle must be aspected by an outer planet transit or progression. Usually there are multiple aspects, but it's only necessary for there to be one to each. For example, there could be an aspect to the progressed Ascendant/Descendant, but not to the natal angle. The same applies to the planets.

- Eclipses (most recent) in aspect to natal or progressed Venus (planet of love)
- Eclipses in aspect to natal or progressed Mars (planet of passion)
- Eclipses in aspect to natal or progressed Ascendant/Descendant (relationship angle)
- Eclipses in aspect to natal or progressed ruler of the natal Descendant
- Eclipses in aspect to natal or progressed ruler of the natal fifth house (romance)
- Eclipses in the natal fifth or seventh houses
- Natal Venus, its aspects and house placement
- Natal Mars, its aspects and house placement
- Natal Ascendant/Descendant and its aspects
- Natal ruling planet of the Descendant, its aspects and house placement
- Natal ruling planet of the fifth house, its aspects and house placement
- Natal planets in the fifth house
- Natal planets in the seventh house
- Progressed Venus, its aspects and house placement
- Progressed Mars, its aspects and house placement
- Progressed Ascendant/Descendant and its aspects
- Progressed ruling planet of the natal Descendant, its aspects and house placement

- Progressed ruling planet of the natal fifth house of romance
- Progressed planets in the fifth house
- Progressed planets in the seventh house
- Outer planets transiting the fifth house
- Outer planets transiting the seventh house
- Outer planets in aspect to natal Venus, Mars, Ascendant/Descendant, and rulers of the Descendant and fifth house
- Outer planets in aspect to progressed Venus, Mars, Ascendant/Descendant, and rulers of the natal Descendant and natal fifth house
- Outer planets in aspect to planets in the fifth or seventh houses
- New or full Moon (most recent) in aspect to natal or progressed Venus
- New or full Moon in aspect to natal or progressed Mars
- New or full Moon in aspect to natal or progressed Ascendant/Descendant
- New or full Moon in aspect to natal or progressed ruler of the Descendant
- New or full Moon in aspect to natal or progressed ruler of the fifth house
- New or full Moon in the natal fifth or seventh house
- Transiting Venus and Mars if in stationary/retrograde pattern
- Transiting rulers of the natal fifth and seventh houses if in stationary/retrograde pattern

All of these planets and angles are, and must be, involved in some way when a major relationship occurs. The Sun (self) and the Moon (emotions) are generally involved as well, but in themselves do not indicate a relationship. Neptune, the ultimate planet of romance, is often involved, either natally or by transit or progression.

It is the Ascendant/Descendant, the relationship axis, that is usually the first tip-off of a serious commitment. Watch for years when the progressed Ascendant/Descendant aspects natal or progressed planets, especially Venus, Mars, and the fifth- and seventh-house rulers. Saturn, Uranus, Neptune, or Pluto in action aspect to the natal Ascendant/Descendant also signal major relationship developments, particularly when stationing there.

Now, let's look at two examples of how this list plays out in real life.

Sudden Love

Charles (chart 15) met the love of his life by chance while working out at the gym. He was in the right place at the right time. Despite the ups and downs found in any close relationship, it lasted for many years.

A true romantic with the Moon in Pisces, a Sun-Neptune square, and Jupiter trine Neptune, Charles searches for the ideal. He has a strong sense of commitment with the Sun and Venus in Taurus.

Here are the pertinent natal and progressed planets:

- Venus, love and fifth-house ruler

- Mars, passion

- Jupiter, natal Descendant ruler

- Uranus, progressed Descendant ruler

Charles met his love on November 26, 1994, at "about noon." The November 3, 1994, solar eclipse at 10°54' Scorpio occurred in the fifth house of romance opposition natal Venus, sesquisquare the natal Moon-Mars conjunction, and semisquare the natal Descendant. The lunar eclipse of November 18, 1994, at 25°42' Taurus activated the natal Sun-Neptune square and sextiled the natal Moon-Mars conjunction. These two eclipses were the new and full Moons that month.

With the eclipses alone, the three appropriate planets—Venus, Mars, and Jupiter—were activated, as were the Ascendant/Descendant relationship axis and the fifth house.

The progressed aspects confirmed the trend indicated by the eclipses:

- Progressed Moon semisquare progressed Venus

- Progressed Moon trine progressed Mars

- Progressed Sun trine natal Moon-Mars conjunction

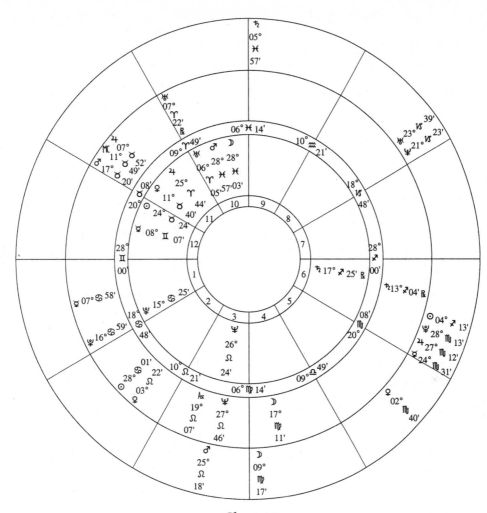

Chart 15
Charles' Progressed Chart with Transits
November 26, 1994 / Placidus Houses

Inner Wheel	**Middle Wheel**	**Outer Wheel**
Birth Chart	Progressed Chart	Transits
May 15, 1928	November 26, 1994	November 26, 1994
7:14 AM EST		

The outer planet transits in aspect to natal and progressed planets/angles were as follows:

- Transiting Jupiter trine natal Moon-Mars conjunction
- Transiting Jupiter square natal/progressed Neptune
- Transiting Jupiter trine progressed Sun
- Transiting Uranus trine natal Sun
- Transiting Pluto trine natal Moon-Mars conjunction
- Transiting Pluto trine progressed Sun

Transiting Venus was a key player in this meeting. It stationed direct three days before they met (November 23, 1994) at 2°29' Scorpio in the fifth house, making this week a likely one for Charles to meet someone special. This is an excellent example of why it's important to glance through the ephemeris when narrowing the time frame for a potential event. Without doing so, you would not have known that Venus was stationing.

The inner planets lined up beautifully on November 26, 1994, a date that could have been predicted with certainty:

- Transiting Moon square natal Mercury (separating) and sesquisquare natal Jupiter (approaching)—The Moon triggered the rulers of the natal Ascendant and Descendant
- Transiting Mercury opposition natal Sun—Triggered natal Sun-Neptune and Jupiter-Neptune aspects
- Transiting Mars conjunct natal/progressed Neptune and trine natal Jupiter—Also triggered natal Sun-Neptune and Jupiter-Neptune aspects
- Transiting Sun trine progressed Venus—Venus, the love planet and ruler of the fifth house
- Transiting Venus in the fifth house square progressed Venus—Venus, the love planet and ruler of the fifth house

In addition to transiting Venus, which had just completed its direct station, the meeting occurred because transiting Mars was activating the above-mentioned natal planets on the same day that the Moon was in the appropriate sign and degree. Note that it was essentially the Moon, Venus, and Mars that triggered the necessary components, each in a different way.

Marriage and Divorce

Film superstar Marilyn Monroe (chart 16) and legendary New York Yankees outfielder Joe DiMaggio (chart 17) were married January 14, 1954, at San Francisco City Hall. She filed for divorce on October 27, 1954, after a tumultuous 274 days. About the marriage, AstroDatabank says, "It was off-key from day one, with two superstars on different tracks, different centers, different values. They fought and screamed, she drank, he hit her."[1]

In addition to the Ascendant/Descendant, Venus, and Mars, the following planets ruled relationships in the two charts:

Marilyn Monroe

Jupiter (natal fifth-house ruler)

Saturn (natal Descendant co-ruler)

Uranus (natal Descendant co-ruler)

Neptune (progressed Descendant ruler)

Natal Moon in the seventh house

Natal Jupiter in the seventh house

Joe DiMaggio

Mars (natal fifth-house ruler)

Mercury (natal Descendant ruler)

Natal Saturn-Pluto conjunction in
   the seventh house

Sun (progressed Descendant ruler)

The solar eclipse of January 4, 1954, at 14°13' Capricorn semisquared Marilyn's natal Jupiter. It was conjunct Joe's progressed Mercury, sextile his natal Mercury, and sesquisquare natal Descendant.

A lunar eclipse occurred at 28°30' Cancer four days after they were married. It squared Marilyn's natal Venus and trined natal Uranus. The same eclipse was sextile Joe's Descendant, conjunct natal/progressed Neptune, and sesquisquare natal Mars.

The eclipses were the new and full Moons that month.

In addition to the progressed Moon in the seventh house and progressed Venus having recently entered Gemini, the progressed aspects to Marilyn's chart were as follows:

- Progressed Moon semisquare progressed Mars
- Progressed Sun semisquare natal/progressed Neptune—Activated the natal seventh-house Moon-Jupiter opposition to Neptune

---

1. AstroDatabank and AstroDatabank.com were developed by the late Lois Rodden, a well-known astrologer who gathered and compiled thousands of pieces of birth data and biographical information on well-known people and other news makers. Her data rating system is the recognized standard for astrological birth data.

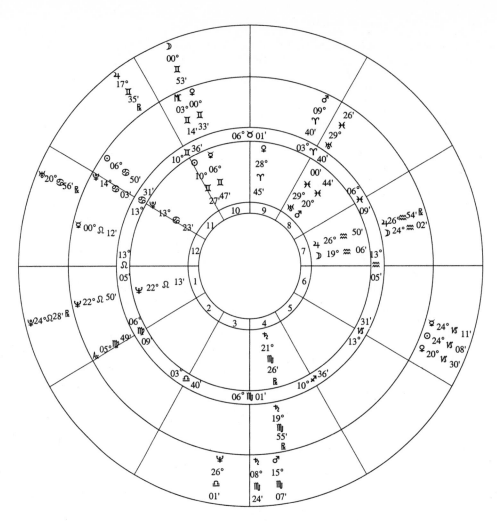

Chart 16
Marilyn Monroe's Progressed Chart with Transits
January 14, 1954 / Placidus Houses

Inner Wheel	**Middle Wheel**	**Outer Wheel**
Birth Chart	Progressed Chart	Transits
June 1, 1926	January 14, 1954	January 14, 1954
9:30 AM PST		
Los Angeles, CA		

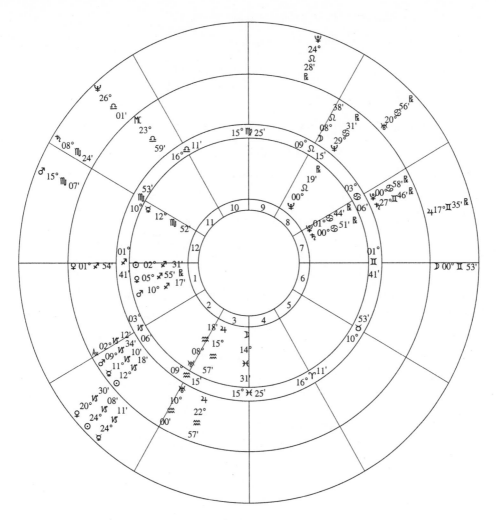

Chart 17
Joe DiMaggio's Progressed Chart with Transits
January 14, 1954 / Placidus Houses

Inner Wheel	**Middle Wheel**	**Outer Wheel**
Birth Chart	Progressed Chart	Transits
November 25, 1914	January 14, 1954	January 14, 1954
7:00 AM PST		
Martinez, CA		

- Progressed Mercury sextile progressed Venus
- Progressed Jupiter conjunct natal Jupiter

Outer planet transits to Marilyn's chart included the following:

- Transiting Uranus trine natal Mars
- Transiting Uranus semisquare progressed Ascendant
- Transiting Neptune trine natal/progressed Jupiter
- Transiting Neptune sesquisquare natal Sun
- Transiting Pluto opposition progressed Moon in the seventh house
- Transiting Pluto opposition natal/progressed Jupiter in the seventh house
- Transiting Pluto conjunct Neptune (although separating, it would station May 4, 1954, at 22°32' Leo)

The outer planet transits involve key marriage planets in Marilyn's chart. However, transiting Pluto's conjunction/opposition to the natal Moon-Jupiter-Neptune configuration in the first/seventh houses is ominous in its potential for an abusive relationship. In this case, it would have been far better to wait until the aspect had passed before she married anyone.

Progressions in Joe's chart were the following:

- Progressed Sun sextile natal Mercury
- Progressed Venus opposition natal Descendant
- Progressed Venus conjunct natal Sun
- Progressed Neptune sesquisquare (exact) natal Moon

Transiting Jupiter, planet of expansion and good fortune, was in Joe's seventh house. Other outer planet transits to Joe's chart were as follows:

- Transiting Saturn square natal Uranus
- Transiting Neptune semisquare natal Mars (stationary retrograde January 27, 1954, at 26°04' Libra)
- Transiting Pluto sesquisquare progressed Mars

When studying transits and progressions and their interaction with natal and progressed planets, it's easy to overlook transiting planets in aspect to each other. The configurations formed by the inner planets (except for the Moon) in aspect to other planets take on added significance when they aspect a natal or progressed planet or angle.

January 14, 1954, was such a day. Transiting Venus opposed transiting Uranus, an aspect under which marriage is inadvisable. The opposition aspected the planets listed below and was triggered by the transiting Moon in the first degrees of Gemini. (Note: Although the exact time of the wedding is unavailable, and the transit chart was therefore calculated for noon, it's reasonable to believe that it took place after the Moon entered Gemini and was conjunct Joe's natal Descendant and Marilyn's progressed Venus.)

Marilyn Monroe

- Transiting Venus sextile and transiting Uranus trine natal Mars
- Transiting Venus sextile and transiting Uranus trine natal Saturn
- Transiting Venus sesquisquare and transiting Uranus semisquare natal Mercury
- Transiting Venus semisquare and transiting Uranus sesquisquare progressed Descendant

Joe DiMaggio

- Transiting Venus semisquare Uranus transiting and Uranus sesquisquare natal Venus (This dual influence involving the same planets is one to watch for. It strengthens both aspects and usually indicates a major event.)

A similar effect was created by the day's transiting Sun-Mercury conjunction:

Marilyn Monroe

- Transiting Sun-Mercury sesquisquare natal Sun

Joe DiMaggio

- Transiting Sun-Mercury semisquare natal Mars

Other inner planet transits aspecting Marilyn's chart were the following:

- Transiting Moon conjunct progressed Venus
- Transiting Mars sesquisquare progressed Uranus

Other inner planet transits aspecting Joe's chart were as follows:

- Transiting Moon conjunct Descendant
- Transiting Moon opposition progressed Venus
- Transiting Mars trine natal Moon
- Transiting Mars square natal Jupiter
- Transiting Mars sesquisquare natal/progressed Saturn-Pluto
- Transiting Mars semisquare progressed Ascendant

11
Job/Career

The sixth and tenth houses govern job/career matters. In general, the sixth house represents a specific job and the work environment; the tenth house is the overall career field. For example, "communication" is a career field in which there are hundreds of different jobs available, from public relations to television to event planning to technical support.

Both the sixth and tenth houses are usually active during a job search. Promotions and career changes almost always require tenth-house activity, such as a progressed or outer transiting planet in action aspect to the Midheaven, the angle associated with career and status.

The importance of the position, as perceived by the individual, also has a bearing on the house activity. While one person might view a particular job offer as a career step, another might consider it "just another job." A recent graduate or unemployed person in search of a job might see an entry-level position as a career opportunity; to someone making a lateral move, it might only be a source of income.

Listed here are the planetary contacts that indicate job/career events. Each must be "active" in some way, whether by progression or outer planet transit. It's particularly important to study the trends, as revealed by progressions and outer planet transits. The best inner planet transits, such as transiting Sun trine natal Saturn, cannot negate the effects of difficult long-term aspects, such as transiting Pluto square natal Saturn.

- Eclipses (most recent) in aspect to natal or progressed Mercury (natural sixth-house ruler)

- Eclipses in aspect to natal or progressed Saturn (career planet)

- Eclipses in aspect to natal or progressed Midheaven (career angle) or their rulers

- Eclipses in aspect to natal or progressed ruler of the natal sixth house

- Eclipses in the natal tenth house

- Natal Mercury, its aspects and house placement

- Natal Saturn, its aspects and house placement

- Natal Midheaven and its aspects

- Natal ruling planet of the Midheaven, its aspects and house placement

- Natal ruling planet of the sixth house, its aspects and house placement

- Natal planets in the sixth house

- Natal planets in the tenth house

- Progressed Mercury, its aspects and house placement

- Progressed Saturn, its aspects and house placement

- Progressed Midheaven and its aspects

- Progressed ruling planet of the natal Midheaven, its aspects and house placement

- Progressed ruling planet of the natal sixth house

- Progressed planets in the sixth house

- Progressed planets in the tenth house

- Outer planets transiting the sixth house

- Outer planets transiting the tenth house

- Outer planets in aspect to natal Mercury, Saturn, Midheaven, and rulers of the Midheaven and sixth house

- Outer planets in aspect to progressed Mercury, Saturn, Midheaven, and rulers of the natal Midheaven and natal sixth house

- Outer planets in aspect to planets in the sixth or tenth house

- New or full Moon in aspect to natal or progressed Mercury

- New or full Moon in aspect to natal or progressed Saturn

- New or full Moon in aspect to natal or progressed Midheaven

- New or full Moon in aspect to natal or progressed ruler of the Midheaven

- New or full Moon in aspect to natal or progressed ruler of the sixth house

- New or full Moon in the natal sixth or tenth house

- Transiting Mercury if in stationary/retrograde pattern

- Transiting Saturn—Focus attention on retrograde/direct stations and multiple transits to the same planets/angles

- Transiting rulers of the natal sixth and tenth houses, especially if in stationary/retrograde pattern

Job Search

John (chart 18) had been unemployed for several years, but when the timing was right, he quickly and easily found an ideal job in the legal field. It was a step up from positions he had initially sought and came together through networking rather than the traditional sources, such as classified ads and the Internet.

His search went beyond a mere job hunt. His ego (Sun, Ascendant, second house) was very much involved, and he referred to the process in terms of "my career" rather than "a job." He also was motivated by financial need (second and eighth houses).

John was offered the job on October 10, 2002, in the "early afternoon" (transits calculated for 1:00 PM), after a friend in another profession connected him with his future employer. He was interviewed and offered the position the same day.

Here are the job/career planets in his chart:

- Midheaven (in Taurus)

- Venus (natal Midheaven ruler)

- Saturn (career planet and natal sixth-house ruler)

- Mercury (natural ruler of the sixth house)

- Moon (progressed Midheaven ruler)

The solar eclipse of June 10, 2002, at 19°54' Gemini in his tenth house was sextile natal/progressed Saturn (sixth-house ruler), opposition progressed Sun (Ascendant

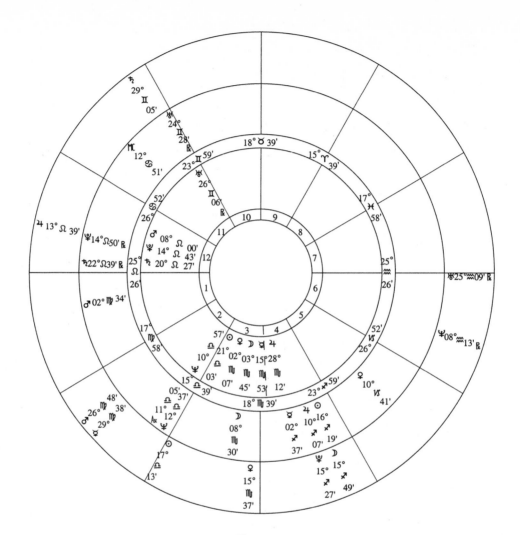

Chart 18
John's Progressed Chart with Transits
October 10, 2002 / Placidus Houses

Inner Wheel	**Middle Wheel**	**Outer Wheel**
Birth Chart	Progressed Chart	Transits
October 15, 1947	October 10, 2002	October 10, 2002
1:29 AM EST		

ruler), and sesquisquare natal Moon-Venus conjunction (Venus is the tenth-house ruler).

The new Moon occurred four days prior to the event, on October 6, 2002, at 13°02' Libra in the second house of money and self-esteem. It was square his progressed Midheaven and conjunct natal/progressed Neptune (ruler of his eighth house of money).

The progressions energized the appropriate planets, as listed here. Many of them also aspected those planets activated by the solar eclipse and new Moon.

- Progressed Moon sesquisquare Uranus (networking)
- Progressed Mercury square Mars
- Progressed Venus square natal Neptune
- Progressed Venus sesquisquare natal Ascendant
- Progressed Midheaven sesquisquare natal Jupiter (luck)

The lucky networking contact that resulted in a job offer is shown in the progressed Moon (progressed Midheaven ruler)–Uranus (networking) and progressed Midheaven-Jupiter aspects, and in transiting Uranus in the sixth house of work within orb of a conjunction to the natal Descendant (other people). Transiting Neptune in the sixth house, which stationed on October 20, 2002, at 8°12' Aquarius, was sesquisquare natal/progressed Uranus, which was triggered by a sesquisquare from the progressed Moon and a square from transiting Mars.

Another outer planet transit that signaled job/career potential was Saturn transiting the eleventh house. It stationed retrograde at 29°05' Gemini on the day of the interview and job offer, where it was sesquisquare natal Mercury (career, networking). Here is the complete list of transiting outer planet contacts that were in effect:

- Transiting Jupiter conjunct Pluto (approaching)
- Transiting Saturn sesquisquare natal Mercury
- Transiting Saturn semisquare natal/progressed Pluto
- Transiting Uranus semisquare progressed Venus
- Transiting Uranus conjunct natal Descendant (approaching)
- Transiting Neptune sesquisquare natal/progressed Uranus
- Transiting Neptune opposition natal Mars
- Transiting Pluto conjunct progressed Sun

A key factor in John's successful job search was a transiting Mercury-Saturn-Venus combination (a transiting Mercury-Saturn square was semisquare/sesquisquare transiting Venus). It worked to his advantage. This three-planet transiting lineup aspected natal Mercury and natal/progressed Pluto (natural ruler of the eighth house of money).

Not to be overlooked was transiting Venus, which stationed retrograde that day at 15°37' Scorpio (and sesquisquare stationing Saturn). The power of the station makes it within orb of an opposition to the natal Midheaven and a favorable trine to the progressed Midheaven. It also was conjunct natal Mercury. Transiting Mars formed a beneficial background aspect as well. It was sextile natal/progressed Jupiter, planet of luck, and also squared natal/progressed Uranus (networking), the ruler of John's seventh house (other people).

These inner planet aspects were in effect:

- Transiting Sun semisquare progressed Mercury
- Transiting Mercury semisquare natal Mercury
- Transiting Mercury semisquare natal/progressed Pluto
- Transiting Venus conjunct natal Mercury
- Transiting Venus square natal/progressed Pluto
- Transiting Venus trine progressed Midheaven
- Transiting Mars sextile natal Jupiter
- Transiting Mars square natal/progressed Uranus

Fame and Fortune

Energetic Bette Midler (chart 19) goes after what she wants with all the pizzazz of her fire sign Ascendant, Sun, Moon, and Mercury. Like most performers who reach star status, her career went through ups and downs in the early years.

Bette found her niche in July 1970, when she was hired to sing at the Continental Baths in New York City, accompanied by the then unknown Barry Manilow. Her popularity rose, and she came to the attention of *The Tonight Show* host Johnny Carson. As Bette's career began to come together, her first album, *The Divine Miss M*, was released just before she appeared at New York City's Lincoln Center Philharmonic Hall on New Year's Eve 1972.

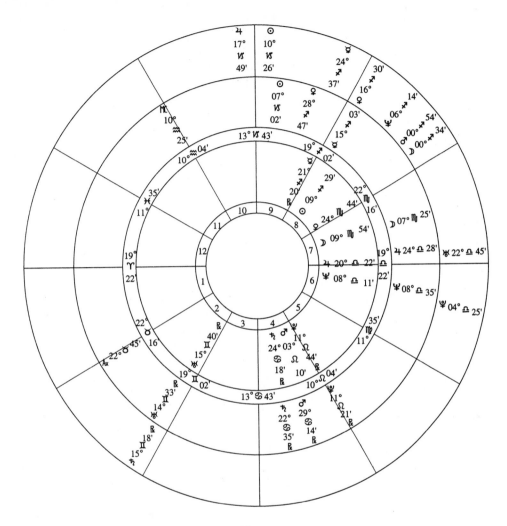

Chart 19
Bette Midler's Progressed Chart with Transits
December 31, 1972 / Placidus Houses

Inner Wheel
Birth Chart
December 1, 1945
2:19 PM HST
Honolulu, HI

Middle Wheel
Progressed Chart
December 31, 1972

Outer Wheel
Transits
December 31, 1972
New York, NY

Bette's job/career planets are the following:

- Saturn (career planet and natal Midheaven ruler)
- Mercury (job planet and natal sixth-house ruler)
- Uranus (progressed Midheaven ruler)
- Transiting Jupiter in the tenth house
- Natal/progressed Neptune in the sixth house
- Transiting Pluto in the sixth house

Four eclipses—two in July 1972 and two in January 1973—set the trend for fame and fortune. Each aspected the career points in her chart:

- Solar eclipse, July 10, 1972, at 18°37' Cancer, opposition natal Midheaven
- Lunar eclipse, July 26, 1972, at 3°24' Aquarius, in the tenth house, opposition natal Mars (Ascendant ruler); and semisquare/sesquisquare natal Sun-Uranus opposition in the second and eighth houses of money (Uranus is the progressed Midheaven ruler)
- Solar eclipse, January 4, 1973, at 14°10' Capricorn, conjunct natal Midheaven
- Lunar eclipse, January 18, 1973, at 28°40' Cancer, conjunct natal/progressed Saturn (Midheaven ruler); square progressed Jupiter (luck); sesquisquare/semisquare natal Sun-Uranus opposition in the second and eighth houses of money (Uranus is the progressed Midheaven ruler); and conjunct progressed Mars

On December 31, 1972, transiting Saturn was conjunct natal/progressed Uranus, which had been aspected by two of the eclipses.

The December 5, 1972, new Moon at 13°49' Sagittarius further activated Bette's natal Sun-Uranus opposition and progressed Mars. The full Moon of December 20, 1972, at 26°37' Gemini opposed progressed Venus, semisquared natal/progressed Pluto, and sesquisquared the progressed Midheaven.

With this stellar backdrop of eclipses and new and full Moons, all that was necessary was for the progressions and outer and inner planet transits to fall into place.

Progressed Mercury added its emphasis to the natal Sun-Uranus aspect through its opposition to natal/progressed Uranus, to which transiting Saturn formed a conjunction; Mercury also sesquisquared progressed Mars, the Ascendant ruler. The progressed

Moon (the public) sextiled the progressed Sun, and the progressed Midheaven squared the natal Moon. The progressed Ascendant sextile progressed Saturn linked Bette (Ascendant) with career success (Saturn, Midheaven ruler), and progressed Jupiter square natal Saturn added luck (natal Venus-Saturn trine).

The active progressed aspects were as follows:

- Progressed Sun sesquisquare progressed Ascendant
- Progressed Moon sextile progressed Sun
- Progressed Mercury sesquisquare progressed Mars
- Progressed Mercury opposition natal/progressed Uranus
- Progressed Jupiter square natal Saturn
- Progressed Ascendant sextile progressed Saturn
- Progressed Midheaven square natal Moon
- Progressed Midheaven opposition natal/progressed Pluto

Lucky Jupiter transiting the tenth house and squaring the Ascendant all but ensured success, especially with the added emphasis of transiting Uranus approaching a stationary conjunction with natal/progressed Jupiter. Jupiter-Uranus is one of the luckiest planetary combinations, and it was triggered that night by a sextile from transiting Mercury.

These were the outer planet transits to progressed and natal planets and angles:

- Transiting Jupiter in the tenth house
- Transiting Jupiter square natal Ascendant
- Transiting Saturn conjunct natal/progressed Uranus
- Transiting Saturn semisquare progressed Mars
- Transiting Uranus conjunct natal/progressed Jupiter (stationary retrograde on January 27, 1973, at 23°04' Libra)
- Transiting Pluto sextile natal Mars (stationary retrograde on January 6, 1973, at 4°26' Libra)

The inner transiting planets added their triggering effect with two aspects to the natal Midheaven and one to the progressed Midheaven. The transits are calculated for 7:00 PM because it was an evening performance.

- Transiting Sun sextile natal Moon
- Transiting Sun sextile natal Venus
- Transiting Moon semisquare natal Midheaven
- Transiting Mercury sextile progressed Jupiter
- Transiting Mercury semisquare progressed Midheaven
- Transiting Mars semisquare natal Midheaven

12
Money

Money ebbs and flows. It's as cyclical as relationships, employment, and personal needs and interests. An even, steady income is, for most people, at times interspersed with periods of less or more. Financial loss threatens security; financial gain is empowering.

The natal chart reveals earning potential, as well as spending habits, plus the chance for a big win or inheritance. Where one person takes a calculated risk that pays off, another is prone to loss through foolish investments or a spendthrift attitude. Some people attract money with ease, while others struggle for every penny.

A financially conservative person with a nest egg can more easily weather lean times, whereas someone else might have to file bankruptcy. Winnings are similar. Financial luck comes in varying degrees, depending on the natal chart. Some people never win a dime, some win small amounts, and a rare few win millions.

Keep these factors in mind when predicting financial gain and loss, and remember that it's all relative to the individual's perspective.

In this chapter, we'll look at the charts of a woman who received an unexpected inheritance, a person who won one million dollars from a slot machine, and a former governor who declared bankruptcy.

The second and eighth are the money houses. In general, the second house governs personal resources, spending, and income, and the eighth house rules joint resources, including debt and inheritance. However, transits and progressions to either house have an overall effect on finances.

The planets that rule financial trends and events are Venus (money planet and natural ruler of the second house), Pluto and Mars (co-rulers of the eighth house), and those that rule the individual chart's second and eighth houses. It's necessary, however, to look beyond these planets and the second and eighth houses to determine the event that brings money matters to the forefront. For example, strong aspects to the sixth and tenth houses could indicate a salary increase or job loss, while those involving the fifth house might reflect a lucky win.

Listed here are the planetary contacts to study when analyzing a chart for finances. Be alert to outer planets transiting the second and eighth houses and progressions that signal current and coming trends.

- Eclipses (most recent) in aspect to natal or progressed Venus
- Eclipses in aspect to natal or progressed Mars
- Eclipses in aspect to natal or progressed Pluto
- Eclipses in aspect to natal or progressed ruler of the natal second house
- Eclipses in the natal eighth house
- Natal Venus, its aspects and house placement
- Natal Mars, its aspects and house placement
- Natal Pluto, its aspects and house placement
- Natal ruling planet of the second house, its aspects and house placement
- Natal ruling planet of the eighth house, its aspects and house placement
- Natal planets in the second house
- Natal planets in the eighth house
- Progressed Venus, its aspects and house placement
- Progressed Mars, its aspects and house placement
- Progressed Pluto, its aspects and house placement (usually the same as natal Pluto because of its slow movement)

- Progressed ruling planet of the natal second house, its aspects and house placement
- Progressed ruling planet of the natal eighth house, its aspect and house placement
- Progressed planets in the second house
- Progressed planets in the eighth house
- Outer planets transiting the second house
- Outer planets transiting the eighth house
- Outer planets in aspect to natal Venus, Mars, Pluto, and rulers of the second and eighth houses
- Outer planets in aspect to progressed Venus, Mars, Pluto, and rulers of the natal second and eighth houses
- Outer planets in aspect to planets in the natal second or eighth houses
- New or full Moon in aspect to natal or progressed Venus
- New or full Moon in aspect to natal or progressed Mars
- New or full Moon in aspect to natal or progressed Pluto
- New or full Moon in aspect to natal or progressed ruler of the second or eighth house
- New or full Moon in the natal second or eighth house

Inheritance

Mary (chart 20) received an unexpected inheritance after her father's death. Unknown to her and her siblings, he had purchased an insurance policy that provided the heirs with $25,000 each.

In addition to a Uranus contact to reflect the windfall, these planets had to be active in Mary's chart natally or by progression or transit:

- Venus
- Mars
- Pluto
- Mercury (second-house ruler)
- Jupiter (eighth-house ruler)

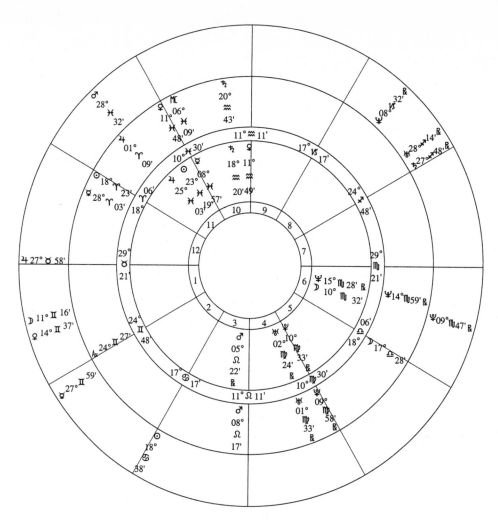

Chart 20
Mary's Progressed Chart with Transits
July 10, 1988 / Placidus Houses

Inner Wheel
Birth Chart
March 14, 1963
9:10 AM CST

Middle Wheel
Progressed Chart
July 10, 1988

Outer Wheel
Transits
July 10, 1988

Before looking at predictive techniques, let's look for the inheritance potential in the natal chart. The Sun and Saturn traditionally rule the father, and the fourth house rules father/parents.

Uranus is in the fourth house of father/parents opposition Mercury (second-house ruler) in an out-of-sign square to the Ascendant and sesquisquare Jupiter (eighth-house ruler) and the Sun (father, fourth-house ruler). This combination of natal aspects links Mary (Ascendant), her father (Sun as ruler of the fourth house and Uranus in the fourth house), his money (eighth house of other people's money), and her money (Mercury as ruler of the second house), suggesting a family inheritance. Why did these aspects, which would appear to block an inheritance, instead promise one?

Looking further, there are several positive natal aspects. Second-house ruler Mercury also trines the Moon (natural fourth-house ruler). The Sun-Jupiter conjunction is lucky, and particularly so for Mary because it links Jupiter (eighth-house ruler) with her father, ruled by the Sun. The Sun rules her natal fourth house, and Jupiter sesquisquares the natal IC.

Mary received news of the inheritance on July 10, 1988. The solar eclipse of March 17, 1988, at 27°42' Pisces was conjunct her natal Sun-Jupiter conjunction and, of course, also activated the natal planets in aspect to Sun-Jupiter.

The new Moon in effect at the time of the inheritance occurred on June 14, 1988, at 23°32' Gemini square natal Sun-Jupiter and conjunct the progressed Ascendant, which would soon enter the second house. The full Moon on June 29, 1988, at 8°15' Capricorn was in the eighth house of inheritance sextile natal Moon (natural fourth-house ruler) and Mercury (second-house ruler).

The progressions echo the influence, with the progressed Moon opposition progressed Sun (fourth-house ruler), trine natal Saturn (father), and semisquare natal Uranus (the unexpected). Progressed Mars (money planet) was sesquisquare natal Sun. Here is the list of active progressions:

- Progressed Sun sextile natal Saturn
- Progressed Moon opposition progressed Sun
- Progressed Moon trine natal Saturn
- Progressed Moon semisquare natal Uranus
- Progressed Venus semisquare progressed Mercury
- Progressed Ascendant on the second-house cusp

The outer planet transits were a major influence. Lucky Jupiter, ruler of Mary's natal eighth house, was sextile natal/progressed Jupiter and approaching natal Ascendant. Uranus, transiting the eighth house, trined progressed Mercury, a background aspect that was aspected by transiting Mercury in the second house. Another particularly significant aspect was transiting Pluto conjunct natal Moon; Pluto was slowing to station on July 20, 1988, at 9°47' Scorpio.

Saturn, transiting the eighth house along with Uranus and Neptune, also trined progressed Mercury (transiting Saturn-Uranus conjunction). Neptune sextiled natal Mercury, revealing the well-kept secret of the inheritance.

Aspects from the transiting outer planets were as follows:

- Transiting Saturn in the eighth house
- Transiting Uranus in the eighth house
- Transiting Neptune in the eighth house
- Transiting Jupiter sextile natal/progressed Jupiter
- Transiting Jupiter conjunct natal Ascendant (approaching)
- Transiting Saturn trine progressed Mercury
- Transiting Uranus trine progressed Mercury
- Transiting Neptune sextile Mercury
- Transiting Pluto conjunct natal Moon
- Transiting Pluto sesquisquare progressed Ascendant

The most significant inner planet triggers were Mercury and Mars. Mercury was separating from a square to natal Jupiter and approaching a square to progressed Jupiter. Mars was doing the same by conjunction. By degree, both planets were almost exactly halfway between natal/progressed Jupiter, a place that is usually a "hot spot" and sensitive to transiting planets. (This technique is valid for all natal/progressed planets.)

The transits shown here were calculated for noon since the exact time is unavailable. They set off planets activated by the March eclipse, new and full Moons, progressions, and outer planet transits:

- Transiting Sun square progressed Sun
- Transiting Mercury sextile progressed Mercury

- Transiting Mercury sextile natal/progressed Jupiter
- Transiting Mars conjunct natal/progressed Jupiter

Million-Dollar Slot Winner

With a pull of the handle, this slot machine player (chart 21) became an instant millionaire on July 18, 1981, at 12:45 AM.

Natally, Venus opposes Pluto from the eighth house to the second house, an aspect that in this chart suggests the potential for a major windfall. Pluto is usually involved in big money. Both planets in background aspect to natal Neptune ease the effect of the opposition. In this chart, Pluto rules the fifth house of gambling, and Mars trine Jupiter is an aspect of good fortune.

Besides Jupiter for luck and Uranus for the surprise, the following are the key planets that had to be active natally or by progression or transit:

- Venus
- Mars
- Pluto (money planet and fifth-house ruler)
- Sun (second-house ruler)
- Saturn (co-ruler of the eighth house)
- Uranus (co-ruler of the eighth house)

The lunar eclipse of July 16, 1981, at 24°31' Capricorn was conjunct natal Sun, and the July 1, 1981, new Moon at 9°50' Cancer squared natal/progressed Mars.

All the necessary planets except Mars, which was energized by the new Moon, were involved in active progressed aspects. Jupiter lives up to its reputation for luck here, and its aspects are a great example of the natal chart unfolding and fulfilling its promise. Jupiter had progressed to a conjunction with natal Venus at the same time that Mars was retrograding into a trine with natal Jupiter (Mars was direct at birth, moved forward, stationed, and turned retrograde).

- Progressed Sun in the eighth house
- Progressed Jupiter in the eighth house
- Progressed Ascendant in the second house

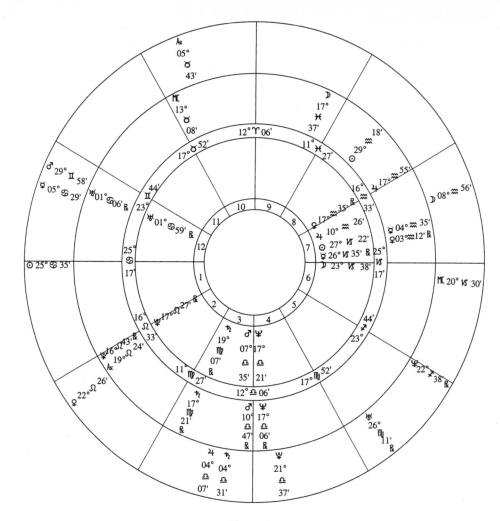

Chart 21
Slot Winner's Progressed Chart with Transits
July 18, 1981 / Placidus Houses

Inner Wheel	**Middle Wheel**	**Outer Wheel**
Birth Chart	Progressed Chart	Transits
January 17, 1950	July 18, 1981	July 18, 1981
4:54 PM PST		

- Progressed Moon opposition natal/progressed Saturn
- Progressed Moon semisquare progressed Venus
- Progressed Mercury conjunction progressed Venus (separating)
- Progressed Mercury sesquisquare natal Saturn
- Progressed Venus sesquisquare natal Saturn
- Progressed Mars trine natal Jupiter (approaching)
- Progressed Jupiter conjunct Venus (separating)
- Progressed Jupiter opposition natal/progressed Pluto (separating)

The transiting outer planets contributed their share of luck, with a Jupiter-Saturn conjunction semisquare the progressed Ascendant in the second house. Transiting the fifth house were Neptune and Uranus, which semisquared progressed Mars (eclipse contact) and sesquisquared the natal Midheaven, the angle associated with fame.

- Transiting Uranus in the fifth house
- Transiting Neptune in the fifth house
- Transiting Jupiter semisquare progressed Ascendant
- Transiting Saturn semisquare progressed Ascendant
- Transiting Uranus semisquare progressed Mars (Uranus stationary direct on August 4, 1981, at 26°03' Scorpio)
- Transiting Uranus sesquisquare natal Midheaven

The inner planet transits triggered all the appropriate planets, and because the winning time is available, so is the exact position of the Moon and the transiting Ascendant and Midheaven. All three were key factors in creating ideal conditions for the win.

The Moon set off the progressed Mars–natal Jupiter trine with its separating trine to Mars and approaching conjunction to Jupiter. The transiting Ascendant was separating from a square to progressed Mercury-Venus and a sesquisquare to natal Saturn, and the transiting Midheaven also aspected natal Saturn (separating trine) as it approached a conjunction to natal Moon.

This chart is also a good example of how Mars acts early. It was approaching a conjunction to natal Uranus, which squares Mars in the natal chart. The transiting Moon, through its aspects to natal Mars and Jupiter, triggered the entire configuration that involved natal Mars, Venus, Uranus, and Pluto (Mars square Uranus, and Uranus sesquisquare/semisquare Venus opposition Pluto). Natal Mars was also energized by a semisquare from transiting Venus in the second house.

- Transiting Sun conjunct natal Ascendant
- Transiting Sun opposition natal Mercury
- Transiting Moon trine natal Mars (separating)
- Transiting Moon conjunct natal Jupiter (approaching)
- Transiting Venus semisquare natal Mars
- Transiting Mars conjunct natal/progressed Uranus (approaching)
- Transiting Ascendant square progressed Mercury-Venus conjunction (separating)
- Transiting Ascendant sesquisquare natal Saturn (separating)
- Transiting Midheaven trine Saturn (separating)

Bankruptcy

J. Fife Symington III (chart 22) filed bankruptcy on September 20, 1995, having previously resigned as governor of Arizona. The bankruptcy was related to financial deals, some of which led to a criminal conviction that was later overturned. He was pardoned by President Clinton before Clinton left office.

Here are Symington's financial planets:

- Venus
- Mars
- Pluto
- Mercury (in the second house, which it rules)
- Jupiter (co-ruler of the eighth house)
- Neptune (co-ruler of the eighth house)

A solar eclipse prior to the bankruptcy filing signaled that financial matters were on the horizon. It occurred on April 29, 1995, at 8°56' Taurus, sextile natal Venus and trine progressed Venus.

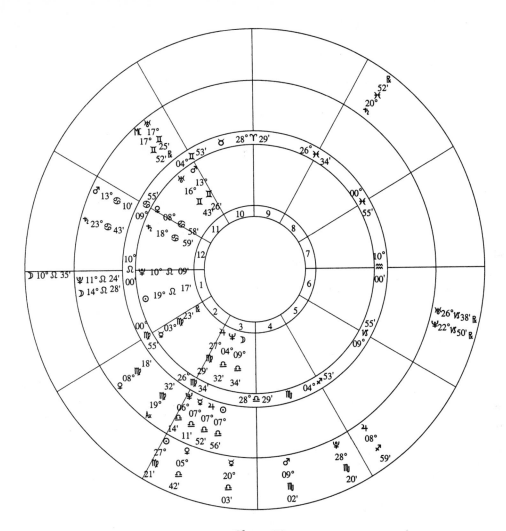

Chart 22
J. Fife Symington's Progressed Chart with Transits
September 20, 1995 / Placidus Houses

Inner Wheel
Birth Chart
August 12, 1945
5:20 AM EWT
New York, NY

Middle Wheel
Progressed Chart
September 20, 1995

Outer Wheel
Transits
September 20, 1995
Phoenix, AZ

The new Moon of August 25, 1995, at 2°29′ Virgo was in his second house conjunct natal Mercury (second-house ruler). The full Moon at 16°00′ Pisces on September 8, 1995, was in his eighth house square natal/progressed Uranus and the progressed Midheaven.

Although there were few progressions active at the time, those that were in effect were powerful and telling. Four progressed planets—Sun, Mercury, Jupiter, and Neptune—formed a stellium that was approaching a square to natal Venus, the lead planet (Sun) only two minutes from a one-degree orb. At the same time, progressed Venus was sextile natal Venus and semisquare progressed Saturn.

Based on the progressions alone, this lineup, in combination with the eclipses and new and full Moons, looks more like a financial windfall. It could have taken the form of a significant salary increase (Saturn, ruler of the sixth house; full Moon square progressed Midheaven) or inheritance (Venus, ruler of the fourth house). The outer planet transits clarify that it was the opposite. Instead, it freed him of debt.

Although Saturn was transiting the eighth house, this is not an indication of bankruptcy in itself. Saturn's transit through the eighth house usually signals a period when every dollar is "hard earned," and some people work two jobs. It's also a time when many pay down or restructure debt. In this case, Symington's debt was "erased" through the bankruptcy proceedings.

Transiting Saturn in the eighth house approaching a trine to itself looks positive, as do transiting Jupiter square progressed Venus and sextile natal Moon, and the lucky transiting Uranus–natal Jupiter trine. But Jupiter also sesquisquares progressed Saturn, and transiting Saturn is approaching a conjunction with the progressed Descendant. Even these hard aspects, however, are not enough to indicate bankruptcy.

The big picture becomes far more negative when aspects from transiting Neptune and Pluto are included. At the time, Neptune opposed progressed Saturn and sesquisquared progressed Venus, and Pluto sesquisquared progressed Mars. Money matters were confusing and beyond Symington's control, yet the influence of lucky Jupiter helped bail him out of his financial difficulties.

The outer planet transits were the following:

- Transiting Jupiter sextile natal Moon
- Transiting Jupiter square progressed Venus
- Transiting Jupiter sesquisquare progressed Saturn

- Transiting Saturn opposition progressed Ascendant (approaching)
- Transiting Saturn trine natal Ascendant (approaching)
- Transiting Uranus trine natal Jupiter
- Transiting Neptune opposition progressed Saturn
- Transiting Neptune sesquisquare progressed Venus
- Transiting Pluto sesquisquare progressed Mars

The inner planet transits are listed below. Notice how they triggered the progressed Sun-Mercury-Jupiter-Neptune stellium and aspects involving Pluto, which is usually active during a bankruptcy. The decision to file bankruptcy was obviously made prior to this date. Transits are for noon, since the exact time is unavailable.

- Transiting Moon conjunct natal/progressed Pluto
- Transiting Sun semisquare progressed Pluto
- Transiting Venus conjunct progressed Sun-Mercury-Jupiter-Neptune conjunction
- Transiting Mars sextile progressed Venus
- Transiting Mars square natal Pluto
- Transiting Mars trine natal Venus

13
Relocation

Millions of people move each year, some locally, some cross-country. Predictive astrology can be a useful tool in determining when relocation will occur. But the trends and aspects that indicate a potential move can also signal remodeling, redecorating, or roommates and relatives moving in or out. Sometimes there's more than one event, such as acquiring a smaller house after a young adult leaves home. Individual life circumstances are usually the best guideline.

Any of the outer planets moving back and forth across the natal or progressed IC (fourth-house cusp) in a retrograde pattern can signal multiple moves, various stages in a renovation project, or buying and selling property. The same things sometimes happen when outer planets cross the natal or progressed Midheaven because its opposite point is the IC.

In addition to the relocation planets and aspects listed below, Saturn is sometimes involved with real estate deals, and eighth-house aspects are common when a home purchase depends on a mortgage. Venus and the second house are usually active as well, because they rule possessions that must be moved.

- Moon (natural fourth-house ruler; the transiting Moon moves too fast to be a relocation indicator)

- Natal fourth-house ruler
- Eclipses in aspect to natal or progressed Moon
- Eclipses in aspect to natal or progressed ruler of the natal fourth house
- Eclipses in the natal fourth house
- Natal Moon, its aspects and house placement
- Natal ruling planet of the fourth house, its aspects and house placement
- Natal planets in the fourth house
- Progressed Moon, its aspects and house placement
- Progressed ruling planet of the natal fourth house, its aspects and house placement
- Progressed planets in the natal fourth house
- Outer planets transiting the natal fourth house
- Outer transiting planets in aspect to natal Moon and natal fourth-house ruler
- Outer transiting planets in aspect to progressed Moon and natal fourth-house ruler
- Outer transiting planets in aspect to planets in the natal fourth house
- New or full Moon in aspect to natal or progressed Moon
- New or full Moon in aspect to natal or progressed ruler of the fourth house
- New or full Moon in the natal fourth house

Home Purchase

Vianne (chart 23) purchased her first home on May 31, 1999, and moved in two months later. Here are the natal and progressed relocation planets in her chart:

- Moon (natal, progressed)
- Venus (possessions and fourth-house ruler)
- Saturn (real estate purchase)
- Sun (second-house ruler; progressed Sun in the fourth house)
- Uranus (eighth-house ruler)
- Jupiter (in the natal fourth house, progressed IC ruler)
- Neptune (in the natal fourth house)

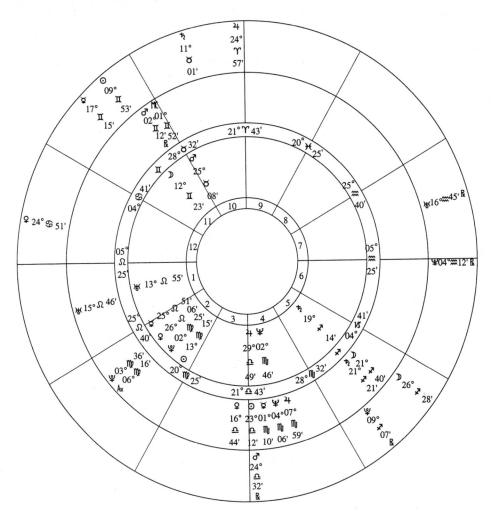

Chart 23
Vianne's Progressed Chart with Transits
May 31, 1999 / Placidus Houses

Inner Wheel	**Middle Wheel**	**Outer Wheel**
Birth Chart	Progressed Chart	Transits
September 6, 1958	May 31, 1999	May 31, 1999
2:35 AM CST		

Two eclipses occurred prior to the purchase and another between the purchase and move-in dates:

- Lunar eclipse, January 31, 1999, at 11°20' Leo, conjunct Uranus and square progressed Jupiter in the fourth house

- Solar eclipse, February 15, 1999, at 27°08' Aquarius, in the eighth house, opposition natal Mercury-Venus conjunction

- Lunar eclipse, July 28, 1999, at 4°58' Aquarius, square fourth-house natal and progressed planets, semisquare natal/progressed Saturn and progressed Moon

The new Moon on May 15, 1999, at 24°14' Taurus squared the natal Mercury-Venus conjunction. Two days before Vianne's home purchase, the full Moon at 8°26' Sagittarius semisquared the progressed Sun in the fourth house.

The progressed Sun in the fourth house is a major indicator of a move. In this chart, it's also a good example of timing. It would have been easy to assume that Vianne would relocate eighteen months earlier when the progressed Sun first entered the fourth house. Why didn't she? For two reasons: because other planetary configurations weren't in agreement, and because she used the energy of the progressed Sun in opposition to the Midheaven to find a new job that would generate the income necessary for home ownership.

By the time of the purchase, the progressed Moon had moved forward to sextile progressed Saturn and progressed Sun. (During the two-month time frame from purchase to move-in, the progressed Moon traveled from 21°42' to 24°03' Sagittarius.) It also semisquared progressed Jupiter in the fourth house.

Three other progressions lined up perfectly: progressed Saturn sextile natal IC, progressed Venus semisquare progressed IC and sesquisquare progressed Mars, and progressed Mars opposition progressed IC was within nine minutes of exact on the day she moved in.

Here are the progressed aspects:

- Progressed Sun in the fourth house
- Progressed Moon sextile progressed Sun
- Progressed Moon semisquare progressed Jupiter
- Progressed Moon conjunct progressed Saturn
- Progressed Venus semisquare progressed IC

- Progressed Saturn sextile natal IC
- Progressed IC opposition progressed Mars

There was a transiting t-square the day Vianne purchased the property: retrograde Mars opposition Jupiter, with Venus squaring both planets. This configuration aspected the fourth-house progressed Sun, activating the full Moon's influence. Transiting Pluto semisquare progressed Sun had as much to do with transforming Vianne's living space and securing a mortgage (Pluto is the natural ruler of the eighth house) as it did re-defining herself as a stable homeowner. The Uranus-Uranus opposition also promoted personal change (natal Uranus in the first house), as is common with this "mid-life cri-sis" aspect that occurs at about the same time for everyone as transiting Neptune squares natal Neptune.

The outer planet transits active on the day she purchased the house are listed here with the pertinent move-in day aspects in parentheses.

- Transiting Jupiter opposition progressed Sun (and opposition progressed Nep-tune, sesquisquare natal Saturn)
- Transiting Jupiter trine natal Mercury-Venus conjunction
- Transiting Saturn trine natal Sun (approaching)
- Transiting Uranus opposition natal Uranus (stationary retrograde on May 21, 1999, at 16°48' Aquarius)
- Transiting Neptune square natal Neptune (stationary retrograde on May 7, 1999, at 4°22' Aquarius)
- Transiting Pluto semisquare progressed Sun

Although transiting retrograde Mars was within three degrees of the natal IC and a little more than a degree from the progressed Sun, it was stationing to turn direct. This and the fact that it was one planet in the transiting t-square strengthened the action and widened the orb.

- Transiting Mercury trine progressed Venus
- Transiting Mercury sesquisquare natal Neptune
- Transiting Venus square progressed Sun

- Transiting Mars conjunct progressed Sun (stationary direct on June 4, 1999, at 24°27' Libra)
- Transiting Mars conjunct natal IC

Double Move

Mary (charts 24 and 25) relocated cross-country on January 21, 1996. She lived in an apartment for about two-and-a-half years before purchasing a house and moving in on August 13, 1998. The relatively short time between the two moves makes this a good big-picture example for comparison and the value of looking ahead for similar trends.

Here are the relocation planets in Mary's chart:

- Sun (fourth-house ruler)
- Moon (natal and progressed)
- Mercury (second-house ruler, progressed IC ruler)
- Venus (possessions)
- Jupiter (eighth-house ruler for the second-move mortgage)
- Saturn (real estate purchase for the second move)
- Uranus (in the natal fourth house)

Like the new and full Moons that occur at about the same degrees for six months of every year, eclipses do the same for several years. The eclipses and new Moons for both moves were in different signs, but within a degree or two of each other.

First Move	Second Move
Lunar eclipse, October 8, 1995, 14°54' Aries	Lunar eclipse, August 7, 1998, 15°21' Aquarius
Solar eclipse, October 23, 1995, 0°18' Scorpio	Solar eclipse, August 21, 1998, 28°48' Leo
New Moon, January 20, 1996, 29°45' Capricorn	New Moon, July 23, 1998, 0°31' Leo

The lunar eclipses aspected the natal IC and progressed Mars. Natal/progressed fourth-house Uranus was aspected by the solar eclipses, and the new Moons connected with the progressed IC. Each of these represents a trend that signals relocation. The progressions continued to advance between the two dates, of which the most notable and telling is progressed Mars.

During the first move, progressed Mars was less than a degree from the natal IC and in an approaching square to natal Moon. By the time of the second move, it was within eight minutes of the natal IC and separating from a square to natal Moon. It also opposed natal Venus. A t-square comprised of natal Moon, progressed Mars, and natal Venus precipitated both moves.

The progressed Moon had just entered the ninth house (long distances) when the first move occurred. At the time of the second move, it was in the tenth house conjunct natal Saturn, reflecting the property purchase. Between the first and second moves, progressed Venus had traveled from a sesquisquare to the natal IC and Mars to a conjunction with the natal Sun, ruler of the fourth house.

The inner and outer planet transits show a similar picture, the most obvious being a transiting planet in place to trigger the Moon-Venus-Mars t-square. It was activated the first time by transiting Mars conjunct Venus, and the second time by transiting Uranus approaching a conjunction to Venus.

During the first move, transiting Uranus was at 0° Aquarius in a wide sesquisquare to the progressed IC that would be well within orb by October 1996, when Uranus stationed direct at the same degree. At the time of the second move, transiting Neptune was at 0° Aquarius, also forming a sesquisquare to the progressed IC; and transiting Uranus opposed the natal IC, a classic relocation aspect.

Transiting Saturn had traveled from a conjunction to progressed Venus, ruler of the Ascendant (moving self and possessions away from family roots, represented by Saturn), to a trine to natal/progressed fourth-house Uranus, thus creating a new, although different, permanent home base.

Transiting Pluto square natal/progressed Uranus at the first move confirms the disruption and disorientation Mary experienced upon leaving her hometown, where she had spent most of her life. By 1998, Pluto was at 5° Sagittarius, trine natal Mars. She used the energy and drive of this aspect to jump into domestic projects that transformed a house into a home.

Besides illustrating how the ever-moving transits and progressions can produce similar energy in different ways, this example shows the importance of looking ahead for

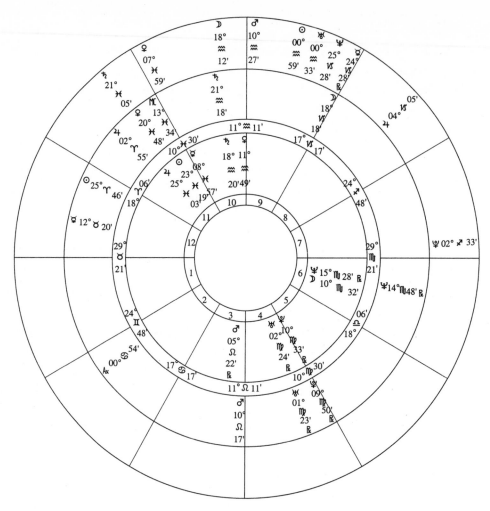

Chart 24
Mary's Progressed Chart with Transits
January 21, 1996 / Placidus Houses

Inner Wheel	Middle Wheel	Outer Wheel
Birth Chart	Progressed Chart	Transits
March 14, 1963	January 21, 1996	January 21, 1996
9:10 AM CST		

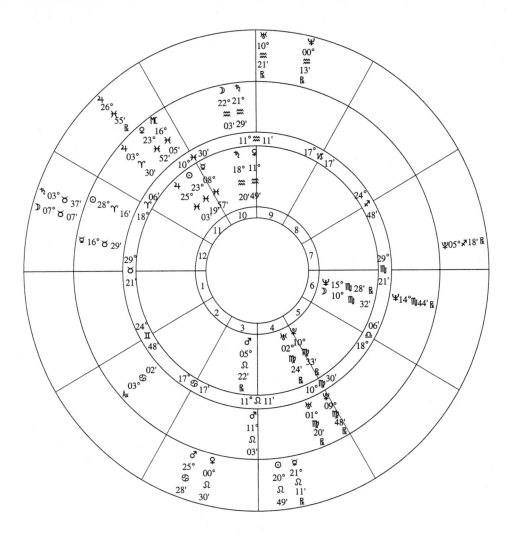

Chart 25
Mary's Progressed Chart with Transits
August 13, 1998 / Placidus Houses

Inner Wheel	**Middle Wheel**	**Outer Wheel**
Birth Chart	Progressed Chart	Transits
March 14, 1963	August 13, 1998	August 13, 1998
9:10 AM CST		

planning purposes. In charts such as this, it would then be possible to prepare for an upcoming home purchase by reducing debt and building savings.

All the aspects for both events are listed below for further study.

First Move

- Progressed Moon in the ninth house
- Progressed Moon sesquisquare natal Uranus
- Progressed Venus sesquisquare natal Mars
- Progressed Venus sesquisquare natal IC
- Progressed Mars square natal Moon
- Transiting Saturn conjunct progressed Venus
- Transiting Saturn sesquisquare natal Mars
- Transiting Neptune square progressed Sun
- Transiting Neptune sextile natal Jupiter
- Transiting Pluto semisquare progressed Moon
- Transiting Pluto square natal Uranus
- Transiting Mercury square progressed Sun
- Transiting Mercury semisquare natal Mercury
- Transiting Venus conjunct natal Mercury
- Transiting Mars square natal Moon
- Transiting Mars conjunct natal Venus
- Transiting Mars opposition progressed Mars
- Transiting Mars opposition natal IC
- Transiting Mars semisquare natal Jupiter
- Transiting Mercury sextile natal Jupiter

Second Move

- Progressed Moon conjunct progressed Saturn
- Progressed Venus conjunct natal Sun

- Progressed Mars square natal Moon
- Progressed Mars opposition natal Venus
- Progressed Mars conjunct natal IC
- Transiting Saturn trine Uranus (stationary retrograde on August 15, 1998, at 3°38' Taurus)
- Transiting Uranus square natal Moon
- Transiting Uranus semisquare natal Jupiter
- Transiting Uranus opposition progressed Mars
- Transiting Uranus opposition natal IC
- Transiting Neptune sesquisquare progressed IC
- Transiting Pluto trine natal Mars
- Transiting Sun-Mercury conjunction in the fourth house
- Transiting Sun-Mercury opposition progressed Moon-Saturn
- Transiting Venus sextile natal Ascendant
- Transiting Venus semisquare progressed IC
- Transiting Mars trine natal Jupiter
- Transiting Mars semisquare Pluto

14
Health

Medical astrology is a highly specialized branch that requires advanced study and experience, and many medical astrologers are also healthcare professionals. Without such study, training, and experience, this is an area in which you should tread lightly.

It is possible, however, to identify planetary configurations that could signal a minor or serious illness. This chapter presents a case study of a man with a common cold.

The sixth and twelfth are the health houses. In general, the sixth house rules overall health and minor upsets, and the twelfth house governs serious or life-threatening conditions. But both houses are usually involved in any health condition.

The fast-moving inner transiting planets on their own can signal a virus or mild infection. However, they also can trigger more serious planetary lineups involving outer planet transits and progressions that involve the twelfth house and more serious concerns. Be cautious and don't jump to conclusions!

In addition to the sixth and twelfth houses and the Sun and Moon (personal planets), these planets are usually active when health is the issue:

- Mercury (natural sixth-house ruler)
- Jupiter (natural twelfth-house ancient ruler)
- Neptune (natural twelfth-house modern ruler)

- Ruling planet of the sixth house
- Ruling planet of the twelfth house
- Planets in the sixth house
- Planets in the twelfth house
- Eclipses (most recent) in aspect to natal or progressed Mercury
- Eclipses in aspect to natal or progressed Jupiter
- Eclipses in aspect to natal or progressed Neptune
- Eclipses in aspect to natal or progressed ruler of the natal sixth house
- Eclipses in aspect to natal or progressed ruler of the natal twelfth house
- Eclipses in the natal sixth house
- Eclipses in the natal twelfth house
- Natal Mercury, its aspects and house placement
- Natal Jupiter, its aspects and house placement
- Natal Neptune, its aspects and house placement
- Natal ruling planet of the sixth house, its aspects and house placement
- Natal ruling planet of the twelfth house, its aspects and house placement
- Natal planets in the sixth house
- Natal planets in the twelfth house
- Progressed Mercury, its aspects and house placement
- Progressed Jupiter, its aspects and house placement
- Progressed Neptune, its aspects and house placement (usually the same as natal Neptune because of its slow movement)
- Progressed ruling planet of the natal sixth house, its aspects and house placement
- Progressed ruling planet of the natal twelfth house, its aspect and house placement
- Progressed planets in the natal sixth house
- Progressed planets in the natal twelfth house
- Outer planets transiting the sixth house
- Outer planets transiting the twelfth house

- Outer planets in aspect to natal Mercury, Jupiter, Neptune, and rulers of the natal sixth and twelfth houses

- Outer planets in aspect to progressed Mercury, Jupiter, Neptune, and rulers of the natal sixth and twelfth houses

- Outer planets in aspect to planets in the sixth or twelfth house

- New or full Moon in aspect to natal or progressed Mercury

- New or full Moon in aspect to natal or progressed Jupiter

- New or full Moon in aspect to natal or progressed Neptune

- New or full Moon in aspect to natal or progressed ruler of the sixth or twelfth house

- New or full Moon in the natal sixth or twelfth house

- Direct/retrograde stations of the outer planets in aspect to the sixth and twelfth houses, Sun, Moon, Mercury, Jupiter, Neptune, and rulers of the sixth and twelfth houses

Common Cold

Phil (chart 26) felt the onset of a cold on the afternoon of October 4, 2002. The cold peaked two days later, and by October 7 he felt well enough to resume normal activities.

The previous solar and lunar eclipses made no health-related aspects. The new Moon of September 6, 2002, at 14°20' Virgo squared the natal Jupiter-Ascendant conjunction. The September 21, 2002, full Moon at 28°25' Pisces sextiled the natal/progressed twelfth-house Saturn-Uranus conjunction and opposed natal Neptune. The lack of eclipse involvement signaled a minor rather than major illness.

It would be easy to predict a major illness based on the progressed Saturn-Uranus conjunction, but this aspect is nothing "new." Phil has lived with this energy his entire life. Had transiting Pluto been stationing there, however, it likely would have indicated far more than a mere cold.

The same could be said of transiting Neptune stationing conjunct Venus, the twelfth-house ruler, and of Saturn stationing square natal/progressed Neptune. All they did, though, was weaken his immune system enough to catch a cold from a co-worker.

Saturn and Capricorn rule colds, and both of them are in evidence in Phil's chart. Besides progressed Saturn being aspected by the full Moon, the transiting Sun was

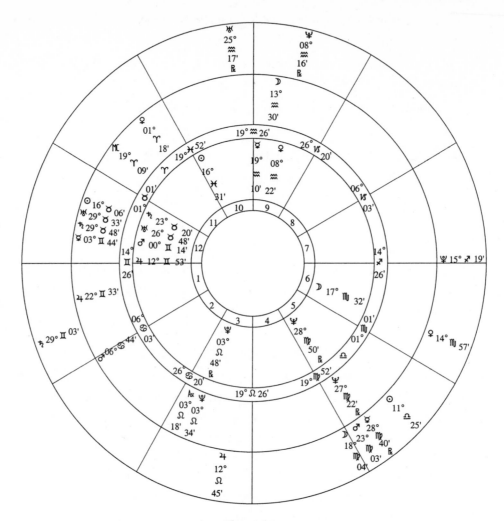

Chart 26
Phil's Progressed Chart with Transits
October 4, 2002 / Placidus Houses

Inner Wheel	Middle Wheel	Outer Wheel
Birth Chart	Progressed Chart	Transits
March 7, 1942	October 4, 2002	October 4, 2002
11:27:30 AM MWT		

sesquisquare the Saturn-Uranus conjunction. A transiting retrograde Mercury-Saturn square formed a conjunction/square to his natal/progressed Neptune. Once Mercury turned direct on October 6, 2002, and the transiting Sun approached a trine to the natal Ascendant, his recovery accelerated.

At the time of the onset of the cold, transiting Mars trined natal Saturn and squared progressed Jupiter, and transiting Sun trined natal Jupiter. Transiting Jupiter in the third house sextiled natal Jupiter and was semisquare natal/progressed Neptune. Since Jupiter rules Phil's sixth house, these aspects probably exposed him to the co-worker's "bug."

Transiting Venus in the sixth house, which was in a transiting sesquisquare with transiting Saturn, was stationing to turn retrograde opposition progressed Sun and within a few degrees of his progressed Moon and natal sixth-house Moon. Had it been exact, it's possible the cold could have hung on for a while. Mars, co-ruler of Scorpio and therefore Phil's sixth house, contacted health planets Venus, Jupiter, and Saturn

These transits were in effect:

- Transiting Sun sesquisquare progressed Saturn
- Transiting Sun sesquisquare natal/progressed Uranus
- Transiting Mercury trine progressed Saturn-Uranus conjunction
- Transiting Mercury conjunct natal/progressed Neptune
- Transiting Venus in the sixth house
- Transiting Venus opposition progressed Sun (stationary retrograde on October 10, 2002, at 15°36' Scorpio)
- Transiting Venus conjunct natal Moon
- Transiting Venus square progressed Moon
- Transiting Mars sesquisquare natal Venus
- Transiting Mars square progressed Jupiter
- Transiting Jupiter sextile natal Jupiter
- Transiting Jupiter semisquare natal/progressed Neptune
- Transiting Saturn square natal Neptune (stationary direct on October 11, 2002, at 29°05' Gemini)
- Transiting Neptune conjunct natal Venus (stationary direct on October 20, 2002, at 8°12' Aquarius)

Glossary

Action Aspect: The square, opposition, semisquare, sesquisquare, and conjunction, depending upon the planets in the conjunction. Action aspects are necessary to set events in motion.

Angle: The Ascendant, Descendant, Midheaven, and IC.

Approaching Aspect: Used in predictive astrology to indicate a faster-moving planet that will soon be within orb to a slower-moving planet.

Ascendant: The first-house cusp. It represents the individual and his or her outward expression of personality.

Aspect: A geometric angle that connects the energy of two or more planets.

Background Aspect: The trine, sextile, and conjunction, depending upon the planets in the conjunction. In predictive astrology, background aspects indicate potential events that can be set into motion by action aspects.

Conjunction: A major action or background (depending upon the planets involved) aspect where two or more planets are close to each other in the zodiac. Its keyword is "intensity."

Degree: The zodiac has 360°, and each sign has 30°. Degrees identify the position of a planet within a sign.

Descendant: The seventh-house cusp, which represents marriage and other close relationships.

Eclipse: Approximately four to six eclipses occur every year. A solar eclipse is also a new Moon, when the Sun and Moon are at the same degree and sign of the zodiac. A lunar eclipse is also a full Moon, when the Sun and Moon are opposite each other.

Element: Each of the twelve signs is classified according to one of the four elements— fire, earth, air, or water.

Full Moon: A full Moon occurs approximately every four weeks, two weeks after the new Moon. The Sun and Moon are opposite each other, 180° apart.

Hemisphere: The four major sections of the horoscope—southern (top half of the chart), northern (bottom half of the chart), eastern (left side of the chart), and western (right side of the chart).

House: One of the twelve pie-shaped sections (houses) of the horoscope. Each house governs specific areas of life.

House Cusp: The sign and degree of the zodiac at which a house begins.

IC (Imum Coeli): The fourth-house cusp. It represents home, family, and parents.

Midheaven: The tenth-house cusp. It represents career and status.

Mode: Each of the twelve signs is identified with one of the three modes of expression —cardinal, fixed, or mutable.

New Moon: A new Moon occurs approximately every four weeks, when the Sun and Moon are at the same degree and sign of the zodiac.

Opposition: A major action aspect where two or more planets are 180° apart, or opposite each other, in the zodiac. It represents "separation."

Orb: The allowable distance between two or more planets that puts them in aspect to one another. The closer the aspect, the stronger its influence.

Quadrants: The four sections of the horoscope that blend the influence of the four hemispheres—first quadrant (houses one, two, and three), second quadrant (houses four, five, and six), third quadrant (houses seven, eight, and nine), and fourth quadrant (houses ten, eleven, and twelve).

Retrograde: The period of time during which planets appear to move backward.

Rulership: Each planet has rulership over, or is associated with, one (or two) signs, and the planet that rules the sign on a house cusp rules that house. Planets and signs also have natural rulership over specific areas of life, such as career, health, family, and money.

Secondary Progressions: A predictive technique that uses the day-for-a-year method of planetary movement.

Semisquare: A minor action aspect where two or more planets are 45° apart. It represents "action" and "conflict."

Separating Aspect: Used in predictive astrology to indicate a planet that has recently moved away from, or out of orb to, another planet.

Sesquisquare: A minor action aspect where two or more planets are 135° apart. It represents "action" and "conflict."

Sextile: A major background aspect where two or more planets are 60° apart. It represents "opportunity."

Square: A major action aspect where two or more planets are 90° apart from each other in the zodiac. It represents "action" and "conflict."

Stationary Planet: The point at which a planet appears to stop before changing to direct or retrograde motion.

Transit: The degree and sign of a planet on a given day.

Trine: A major aspect where two or more planets are 120° apart. It represents "ease" and "luck."

Appendix 1
Step-by-Step Guide
to Making Predictions

Use this step-by-step guide to first do an overview of your natal chart and then to predict trends and events. It's far easier to learn predictive astrology by working with the charts of people you know well. Your own birth chart is the best starting point. Fill in the blanks below with numbers, planets, signs, and aspects, and jot keywords next to each.

Hemispheres

North_____

South_____

East_____

West_____

Quadrants

First_____

Second_____

Third_____

Fourth_____

Elements

Fire_____

Earth_____

Air_____

Water_____

Modes

Cardinal_____

Fixed_____

Mutable_____

Sun

Sign_____

Aspects_____

_____

_____

Moon

Sign_____

Aspects_____

_____

_____

Ascendant

Sign_____

Aspects_____

_____

_____

Dominant Planets

Rising Planet(s)_____

   Aspects_____

       _____

Angular Planet(s)_____

   Aspects_____

       _____

Planets in Close Aspects by Degree_____

_____

Planets in Mutual Reception_____

_____

Major Configurations_____

_____

Ascendant and Midheaven Rulers_____

_____

Strengths   Weaknesses

_____   _____

_____   _____

_____   _____

_____   _____

_____   _____

_____   _____

_____   _____

_____   _____

_____   _____

_____   _____

_____   _____

_____   _____

Eclipses

List the most recent past and approaching eclipses, their dates, and the planets/angles they aspect in your natal chart.

Lunar Eclipse_____

Solar Eclipse_____

Lunar Eclipse_____

Solar Eclipse_____

Lunar Eclipse_____

Solar Eclipse_____

Outer Planet Aspects

List the house each outer planet is transiting and its influence; for example, seventh house is relationships, tenth house is career. Then do the same with the house(s) the transiting planet rules (the planet associated with the sign on the house cusp) in your natal chart and the house that contains the natal planet.

Jupiter

Transit House_____

Natal House_____

Natal House Rulership_____

Saturn

Transit House_____

Natal House_____

Natal House Rulership_____

Uranus

Transit House_____

Natal House_____

Natal House Rulership_____

Neptune

Transit House_____

Natal House_____

Natal House Rulership_____

Pluto

Transit House_____

Natal House_____

Natal House Rulership_____

Now list the active houses and look for the trend(s).

_____

_____

_____

_____

_____

List the outer planet aspects to your natal planets/angles, and jot down keywords for each aspect.

Jupiter_____

_____

_____

Saturn_____

_____

_____

Uranus_____

_____

_____

Neptune_____

_____

_____

Pluto_____

_____

_____

Now do the same for the progressed planets/angles.

Jupiter_____

_____

_____

Saturn_____

_____

_____

Uranus_____

_____

_____

Neptune_____

_____

_____

Pluto_____

_____

_____

Which planets make the most aspects?_____

Which planets are in aspect to progressed-natal aspects?

_____

_____

_____

Which planets are in aspect to progressed-progressed aspects?

_____

_____

Using keywords, list the trend(s) indicated by these aspects.

_____

_____

_____

_____

Now review all you've written. One or two themes should emerge as the strongest. Overall, are they positive or negative? Remember, some action aspects are necessary to spark an event. If you see only action aspects, this is probably not the time to initiate an event such as a marriage or job change. If the indicators are mixed, keep this in mind when looking at the inner planet transits; the outcome could go either way, or you might be able to take advantage of helpful inner planet transits. A mostly positive trend is encouraging for any activity/event and can be initiated by the inner planets.

Inner Planet Transits, New and Full Moons

Review your notes before you begin to look at the new and full Moons and inner planet transits. Start with one trend and identify a specific event connected with it, such as receiving a promotion; getting a new job; starting a new relationship, becoming engaged, or getting married; or buying or renting a new home.

List the houses that apply to the event and their rulers (e.g., sixth and tenth houses for job/career, fifth and seventh houses for relationships).

_____

_____

_____

_____

List the appropriate event planets/angles in your progressed and natal charts. Include planets in the houses identified in the previous question and those that rule them. Note the trend aspects (progressed and outer planet transits) and eclipses next to them.

_____

_____

_____

_____

_____

Now flip through the ephemeris in search of new and/or full Moons that aspect the above planets/angles. Write the date, degree, and sign of the Moon and the aspect it makes.

_____

_____

_____

_____

Focus on the above two- or four-week period (period of influence of the new or full Moon) to begin your search for the inner transiting planets. Start with Mars, the action planet, and move backward though the Sun. Remember, some action aspects (conjunction, opposition, square, semisquare, and sesquisquare) are necessary to generate an event, and some of them must connect with the trend aspects. List the possibilities below, including the specific aspect and date.

Mars_____

_____

_____

_____

Venus_____

_____

_____

_____

Mercury_____

_____

_____

_____

Sun_____

_____

_____

_____

Review your list. Zero in on the dates with the most aspects. They should fall within a two- to three-day time frame, and there may be two such periods. Now look at the Moon's position. Find the date(s) it forms an action aspect to the transiting planets listed above and the important natal and progressed aspects. This date(s) has the highest potential for an event.

You might want to begin with the major aspects (conjunction, trine, sextile, square, opposition), which are easier to spot. Once you've targeted possible dates, add the semisquares and sesquisquares. With a little practice, you'll soon be able to spot likely dates by glancing through the ephemeris.

Now look at the big picture using a triwheel chart. It should have your natal chart in the inner wheel, your progressed chart in the middle wheel, and the transits in the outer wheel. Refer to your aspect lists as you study the charts. If visual cues are helpful to you, use highlighters to mark the aspects.

Are the overall trends positive or negative? Your natal chart and its aspects offer the best clues, followed by the trend aspects and the inner planet triggers. Put your prediction in writing so you can refer to it. Once the event is concluded and you know all the facts, study the charts again. Chances are you'll see things you previously missed. You'll learn as much about predictive astrology as you will about yourself.

You can also use the above steps to predict the outcome of a specific event when you know the scheduled date. Try it for a first date, travel, professional presentation, interview, shopping trip, or any major or minor event.

Appendix 2
Map Your Future
Using the CD-ROM

First you need to install the program. Remove the CD-ROM from its folder and place it in your computer's CD-ROM drive. The program will begin to install itself.

If it does not install automatically, click on the Start menu and select "Run." In the Run menu dialog box, type in your corresponding CD-ROM drive followed by the file name SETUP.exe. Typically, the CD-ROM is set up as D:\. The install wizard will run and guide you through the rest of the process.

For an alternate method, you can access your CD-ROM drive by clicking on "My Computer" and then the CD-ROM drive (typically D:\). Double-click the SETUP.exe icon.

You will see an introductory screen with the name of the program (it flashes on and off very quickly), and then you will see a screen called "Mapping Your Future." This screen is pictured on the following page.

Mapping Your Future is a basic astrology program designed around the most sophisticated astrology programming available. Cosmic Patterns, in collaboration with Llewellyn Worldwide, has developed this program to provide you with birth charts (the circle with all the astrological symbols) and transit interpretations (about ten pages of information about your future). Let's discuss the choices you have on this screen:

- The Start menu is used to create your charts.
- The About menu provides information about the program; about Llewellyn Worldwide, the publisher of *Mapping Your Future*; and about Cosmic Patterns Software, the designer of the program.
- The Quit menu allows you to exit from the program.

Creating Your Chart and Transit Interpretation

To use your program, select "Start" from the menu at the top of the screen, and then select "New List of Charts (New Session)." If you are returning to the program and want to see the last chart you made, select "Continue with Charts of Previous Session."

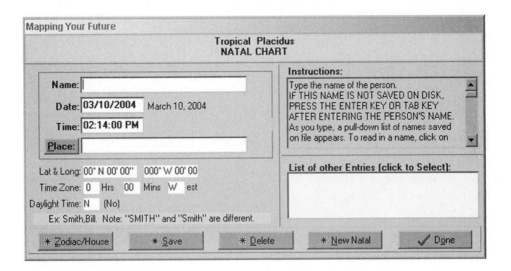

This is where you enter your birth information. There are some simple instructions on the right side of the screen, similar to what follows here. Let's make a chart for Bill Clinton as an example.

- In the Name box, type "Bill Clinton," and Enter.

- In the Date box, type "08191946" (for August 19, 1946), and Enter.

- In the Time field, type "085100 AM" (the birth time of 8:51 AM in "hh mm ss" format), and Enter.

- In the Place box, type "Hope, Arkansas" (the birth place). As soon as you type the word "Hope," a list drops down. You will notice that Hope, Arkansas, isn't in the list, but Hope is close to Texarkana, Arkansas. So instead, begin typing "Texarkana." When you have typed "Tex," Texarkana, Arkansas, will appear at the top of the list. Select it. The drop-down list disappears, and you will see Texarkana, Arkansas, in the Place box. You will also see information filled in the

boxes below it: the latitude is 33N26 00, the longitude is 094W03 00, the time
zone is 6 hours 0 minutes West, and the Daylight Saving Time box is marked "N."

If your city does not automatically come up in the list, you can use a nearby city from
the list, just like we did in this example. You can also look up your birth place in an atlas
to find the latitude and longitude, time zone, and daylight saving time information. A
city close to the birth place is close enough for most purposes and will also be in the
same time zone. If the time zone information is different, your chart could be off by an
hour one way or the other. Depending on the distance your choice is from your actual
birth place, your chart will be slightly different. You can obtain the correct longitude,
latitude, and time information from a Time Table book for astrology.[1]

The Zodiac/House button allows you to select a different house system. The program automatically selects the tropical zodiac and Placidus house system. Experiment
with the other choices to see what changes on the chart wheel.

Select the Save button at the bottom of the screen to save the chart (you can delete it
later if you need to), and then click "OK."

You can enter more than one chart at a time. To do this, click the New Natal button.
The first chart is listed in the window on the right side of the box. Now simply enter the
next chart or type a name for a chart you have already entered, and select from the
drop-down name list.

Then select the Done button. If you forget to save and go directly to the Done button, you will get a prompt asking if you want to save the data. In fact, all the way along
prompts appear to help you enter the data.

After you click the Done button, you will see an information box that says "Enter the
Date." Follow the same procedure for entering the date that you used with the birth information. This time you enter the date on which the interpretation should start. When
you are finished, click "OK." Transits for all charts entered at the same time will begin on
the same date.

---

1. Here are two possibilities: *The American Atlas,* compiled and programmed by Neil F. Michelsen (San
   Diego, CA: ACS Publications, 1978); and *The International Atlas,* compiled and programmed by Thomas
   G. Shanks (San Diego, CA: ACS Publications, 1985).

This is what you see when you click the OK button:

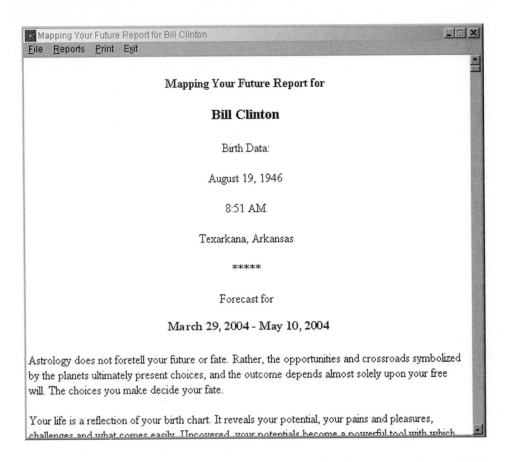

This screen shows the name of the person whose chart you just entered, along with the beginning of the interpretation. As you scroll down, you see a list of dates, aspects, and interpretations.

If you select the word "Wheel" from the Reports menu, a form appears. It contains a birth chart for Bill Clinton, which is pictured on the next page.

To see additional entries, click the "Entries" button at the top of the screen. If only one chart is entered, this button is not visible at the top of the screen.

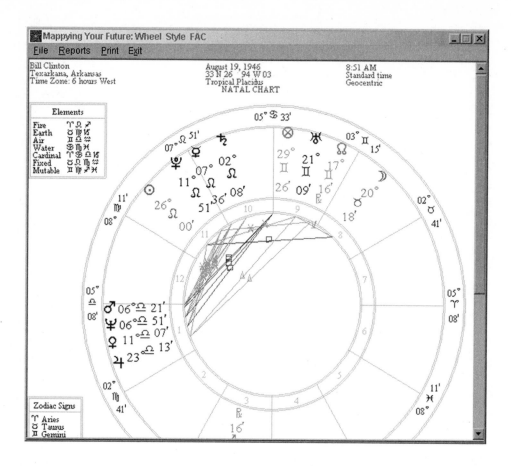

Select "Print" and "Print Current Report" to print either the wheel or the interpretation report. Only the item on the screen prints. Select the other option on the Reports menu to change the screen.

Select "Exit and then "Yes" to go to the opening screen. From here you can either exit the program, or select "Start" to make another chart and forecast.

That's it! You can now create charts and forecasts for any birth information you want. This program is so easy to use that you won't need much help.

Bibliography

Clement, Stephanie Jean, Ph.D. *Mapping Your Birthchart*. St. Paul, MN: Llewellyn Publications, 2002.

George, Llewellyn. *Llewellyn's New A to Z Horoscope Maker and Interpreter*. Revised and expanded by Stephanie Jean Clement, Ph.D., and Marylee Bytheriver. St. Paul, MN: Llewellyn Publications, 2003.

Hand, Robert. *Planets in Transit*. Atglen, PA: Schiffer Publishing, 1976.

Lewi, Grant. *Astrology for the Millions*. St. Paul, MN: Llewellyn Publications, 1990.

———. *Heaven Knows What*. St. Paul, MN: Llewellyn Publications, 1994.

Lineman, Rose. *Eclipse Interpretation Manual*. Tempe, AZ: American Federation of Astrologers, 1986.

Lineman, Rose, and Jan Popelka. *Compendium of Astrology*. Atglen, PA: Schiffer Publishing, 1984.

Pharr, Daniel. *The Moon and Everyday Living*. St. Paul, MN: Llewellyn Publications, 2002.

Rushman, Carol. *The Art of Predictive Astrology*. St. Paul, MN: Llewellyn Publications, 2002.

Tierney, Bil. *Alive and Well with Neptune*. St. Paul, MN: Llewellyn Publications, 1999.

———. *Alive and Well with Pluto*. St. Paul, MN: Llewellyn Publications, 1999.

———. *Alive and Well with Uranus*. St. Paul, MN: Llewellyn Publications, 1999.

———. *The Twelve Faces of Saturn*. St. Paul, MN: Llewellyn Publications, 1997.

☽ LLEWELLYN ORDERING INFORMATION

Order Online:
Visit our website at www.llewellyn.com, select your books, and order them on our secure server.

Order by Phone:
- Call toll-free within the U.S. at 1-877-NEW-WRLD (1-877-639-9753). Call toll-free within Canada at 1-866-NEW-WRLD (1-866-639-9753).
- We accept VISA, MasterCard, and American Express

Order by Mail:
Send the full price of your order (MN residents add 7% sales tax) in U.S. funds, plus postage & handling to:

Llewellyn Worldwide
P.O. Box 64383, Dept. 0-7387-0501-2
St. Paul, MN 55164-0383, U.S.A.

Postage & Handling:

Standard (U.S., Mexico, & Canada). If your order is:
Up to $25.00, add $3.50
$25.01 - $48.99, add $4.00
$49.00 and over, FREE STANDARD SHIPPING
(Continental U.S. orders ship UPS. AK, HI, PR, & P.O. Boxes ship USPS 1st class. Mex. & Can. ship PMB.)

International Orders:
Surface Mail: For orders of $20.00 or less, add $5 plus $1 per item ordered. For orders of $20.01 and over, add $6 plus $1 per item ordered.

Air Mail:
Books: Postage & Handling is equal to the total retail price of all books in the order.
Non-book items: Add $5 for each item.

Orders are processed within 2 business days. Please allow for normal shipping time.
Postage and handling rates subject to change.

ALL AROUND THE ZODIAC

Exploring Astrology's Twelve Signs

Bil Tierney

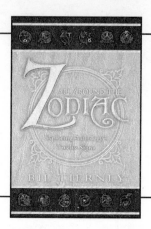

A fresh, in-depth perspective on the zodiac you thought you knew. This book provides a revealing new look at the astrological signs, from Aries to Pisces. Gain a deeper understanding of how each sign motivates you to grow and evolve in consciousness. How does Aries work with Pisces? What does Gemini share in common with Scorpio? *All Around the Zodiac* is the only book on the market to explore these sign combinations to such a degree.

Not your typical Sun sign guide, this book is broken into three parts. Part 1 defines the signs, part 2 analyzes the expression of sixty-six pairs of signs, and part 3 designates the expression of the planets and houses in the signs.

0-7387-0111-4, 528 pp., 6 x 9 $17.95

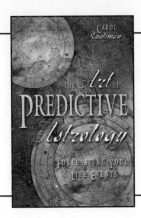

THE ART OF PREDICTIVE ASTROLOGY
Forecasting Your Life Events

CAROL RUSHMAN

Become an expert at seeing the future in anyone's astrological chart! Insight into the future is a large part of the intrigue and mystery of astrology. *The Art of Predictive Astrology* clearly lays out a step-by-step system that astrologers can use to forecast significant events including love and financial success. When finished with the book, readers will be able to predict cycles and trends for the next several years, and give their clients fifteen important dates for the coming year. An emphasis is on progressions, eclipses, and lunations as important predictive tools.

0-7387-0164-5, 288 pp., 6 x 9   **$14.95**

ASTROLOGY
Understanding the Birth Chart

KEVIN BURK

This beginning-to intermediate-level astrology book is based on a course taught to prepare students for the NCGR Level I Astrological Certification exam. It is a unique book for several reasons. First, rather than being an astrological phrase book or "cookbook," it helps students to understand the language of astrology. From the beginning, students are encouraged to focus on the concepts, not the keywords. Second, as soon as you are familiar with the fundamental elements of astrology, the focus shifts to learning how to work with these basics to form a coherent, synthesized interpretation of a birth chart.

In addition, it explains how to work with traditional astrological techniques, most notably the essential dignities. All interpretive factors are brought together in the context of a full interpretation of the charts of Sylvester Stallone, Meryl Streep, Eva Peron, and Woody Allen. This book fits the niche between cookbook astrology books and more technical manuals.

1-56718-088-4, 384 pp., 7½ x 9⅛, illus.   **$17.95**

ASTROLOGY & RELATIONSHIPS
Techniques for Harmonious Personal Connections

DAVID POND

Take your relationships to a deeper level. There is a hunger for intimacy in the modern world. *Astrology & Relationships* is a guidebook on how to use astrology to improve all your relationships. This is not fortunetelling astrology, predicting which signs you will be most compatible with; instead, it uses astrology as a model to help you experience greater fulfillment and joy in relating to others. You can also look up your planets, and those of others, to discover specific relationship needs and talents.

What makes this book unique is that it goes beyond descriptive astrology to suggest methods and techniques for actualizing the stages of a relationship that each planet represents. Many of the exercises are designed to awaken individual skills and heighten self-understanding, leading you to first identify a particular quality within yourself, and then to relate to it in others.

0-7387-0046-0, 368 pp., 7½ x 9⅛ $17.95

THE COMPLETE NODE BOOK
Understanding Your Life's Purpose

KEVIN BURK

This book is the first comprehensive guide to the Moon's Nodes—probably the most misunderstood points in astrology.

While other books on the Nodes make the assumption, for example, that the North Node in Aries is the same thing as the North Node in the first house, this book gives complete interpretations of every sign and house combination. It begins with an overview of the lessons of each Nodal Axis by sign; then addresses the specific lessons and challenges presented by each North Node/South Node combination within that sign; and finally interprets each of the twelve house positions of that specific Node combination.

- Creates a new and empowering understanding of the Nodes, which have not been well-represented in print until now
- Addresses both the higher, constructive expression of the node's energy, along with its lower expression or "trap"
- The only source that completely defines and interprets the Moon's Nodes through all possible combinations of sign and house
- The only integrated interpretations of the Moon's Nodes currently available
- For beginning to advanced astrologers
- Includes an offer for a free birth chart

ISBN 0-7387-0352-4, 240 pp., 6 x 9 $15.95

To order, call 1-877-NEW-WRLD
Prices subject to change without notice

IDENTIFYING PLANETARY TRIGGERS
Astrological Techniques for Prediction

CELESTE TEAL

This technical approach to prediction is for intermediate and advanced astrologers who want to build upon the themes in progressed charts using planetary return charts, transiting aspects, and other little-known but extremely accurate secrets.

One chapter is devoted to each planetary return, from the moon through Saturn, where chart illustrations and commentary lead you step by step through the process. Learn various calculation techniques of the returns, such as whether or not to precess a chart and what the underlying difference is. Several special charts are introduced, including the Anlunar, Sunrise chart, and Diurnal chart.

What's more, the classic reference on transits by Dr. Heber Smith is reprinted in its original form, instilling an understanding of how the transiting planets function. The significance of the nodes of the moon, their transits, and aspects are followed by a table of the nodal positions from 1935 to 2054.

1-56718-705-6, 384 pp., 7½ x 9⅛   **$17.95**

LUNAR RETURNS

JOHN TOWNLEY

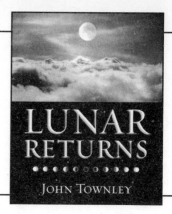

Cast your lunar chart to unravel the surprises and opportunities for the next 27½ days. Each month of your life has its own special dynamic—will it come on like a juggernaut, sneak up like a cat, or stride in like a hero? Find the answer when the transiting Moon hits your natal Moon. This is your lunar return—an emotional rebirthing that occurs every 27½ days.

The lunar return chart exposes the immediate terrain of your life and can guide your day-to-day decisions. It lives in its own right and in relation to the natal chart, and it responds to transits during the month.

This book explores the interpretation of the lunar return in depth. Learn the five significant factors to be delineated through the lunar return chart, and refer to the extensive cookbook-style reference section of houses, aspects, and transits.

0-7387-0302-8, 272 pp., 7½ x 9⅛   **$19.95**

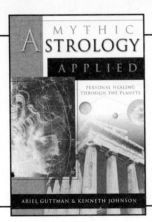

MYTHIC ASTROLOGY APPLIED
Personal Healing Through the Planets

ARIEL GUTTMAN & KENNETH JOHNSON

The gods and goddesses of the ancient world are still with us today. They act out in our celebrities, the media, and most of all within our ourselves—often through our dreams and our own horoscopes. Through the planets in your chart you can discover the mythic dimensions of your own life. The authors of Mythic Astrology provide a way to do just that in their new book, *Mythic Astrology Applied*. Learn how to contact, work with, and bring harmony to the planetary archetypes within yourself.

This book might have you saying things like: "Now I know why I married a Vesta but really long for a Venus as my partner," or "Now I understand my relationship with my mother; she is a Demeter and I'm a Persephone."

0-7387-0425-3, 360 pp., 7 x 10, illus.   **$24.95**

PREDICTIVE ASTROLOGY
A Practical Guide

CHRISTINE SHAW

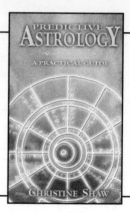

A no-nonsense guide to using progressions to predict the future in someone's life. This book is written for those who have a thorough knowledge of basic astrology and are faced with analyzing progressions, one of the tools astrologers use to predict future trends in someone's life. Without wading through a lot of extraneous material, you will be able to jump right into examining the status of natal planets and then relate that knowledge to the solar arc and secondary progressions methods of predicting future trends. You will explore planets that change direction, natally unaspected planets, stationary and retrograde planets, and planets that change signs and houses when progressed. You will also learn how to read converse predictions, which are interpreted differently from "forwards" progressions.

Predictive Astrology is jampacked with information and tips, including all the pitfalls to avoid and items to remember when progressing a chart. It also includes a chapter on counseling.

0-7387-0045-2, 228 pp., 6 x 9 $14.95

To order, call 1-877-NEW-WRLD
Prices subject to change without notice

More than half-a-million copies sold!

Do your own horoscope

HEAVEN KNOWS WHAT

in just 30 minutes!

Grant Lewi

HEAVEN KNOWS WHAT

GRANT LEWI

Here's the fun, new edition of the classic *Heaven Knows What!* What better way to begin the study of astrology than to actually do it while you learn. *Heaven Knows What* contains everything you need to cast and interpret complete natal charts without memorizing any symbols, without confusing calculations, and without previous experience or training. The tear-out horoscope blanks and special "aspect wheel" make it amazingly easy.

The author explains the influence of every natal sun and moon combination, and describes the effects of every major planetary aspect in language designed for the modern reader. His readable and witty interpretations are so relevant that even long-practicing astrologers gain new psychological insight into the characteristics of the signs and meanings of the aspects.

Grant Lewi is sometimes called the father of "do-it-yourself" astrology, and is considered by many to have been astrology's forerunner to the computer.

0-87542-444-9, 480 pp., 6 x 9, tables, charts   **$14.95**

HEAVEN KNOWS WHAT HOROSCOPE BLANKS
This is the perfect accompaniment to the book. Pack of 50 allows you to cast charts for all of your family and friends.

0-87542-443-2, 8½ x 11   **$3.00**

To order, call 1-877-NEW-WRLD
Prices subject to change without notice